Collins *gem*

Sharks

Dr Geoffrey W. Potts and Silja Swaby
Colour illustrations by Sean Milne

First published in 1997 by Collins, an imprint of HarperCollins*Publishers*
77–85 Fulham Palace Road, London W6 8JB
www.collins.co.uk

This edition first published 1999

10 9 8 7 6 5 4 3 2 1
10 09 08 07 06 05

A catalogue record for this book is available from the British Library

ISBN 0 00 721171 6

Printed and bound by Amadeus S.r.l., Italy

Contents Key

There are about 800 species of sharks and rays in the world. The 207 described in this book are divided into 14 groups, each of which is depicted by a distinctive symbol at the top of the page. A general introduction describes each of the groups, and a selection of species from each group is illustrated and described in more detail. In groups that contain numerous similar species, the species chosen are the best-known and most interesting, and those showing the widest geographical distribution.

While many sharks and rays will bite if provoked, only a few are known to attack humans. These are shown throughout the book by a skull and crossbones symbol.

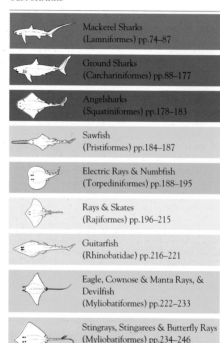

INTRODUCTION

Sharks and rays can inspire, amaze and strike fear into the most courageous of hearts. They are one of the oldest and most diverse groups of vertebrates (animals with backbones), dating back more than 350 million years. The shark's familiar form is instantly recognisable, superbly adapted for life in the world's oceans, the epitome of the mysterious and the majestic.

Many sharks and rays are small, lethargic and insignificant; others are top predators, fast and streamlined with a sensory system able to detect blood in incredibly low concentrations over distances of 2 km. While some scarcely reach 15 cm in length, others are true giants. Indeed, the largest fish in the world is the Whale Shark (p. 72), a gentle monster of 12 m, which filters the seas for plankton. If the Whale Shark is harmless, the Great White (p. 84) certainly is not. It is a voracious predator, reaching 8 m in length, with large, jagged, triangular teeth used to bite and devour its prey. An extinct ancestor, *Charcaradon megalodon*, over 20 m in length and with a jaw gape of over 2 metres, is considered to be the largest predator that ever lived on earth. When presented with such diversity, beauty and awesome power, it is no wonder we are fascinated by these amazing creatures.

WHAT IS A SHARK?

The typical shark is a beautifully streamlined fish, well adapted to life in today's oceans. A close inspection of shark anatomy indicates a number of features that they share with their relatives that lived millions of years ago. One of the ways of identifying sharks and rays is that they have a

Shark anatomy

tail

second dorsal fin

keel

anal fin

lateral line

clasper (male only)

ovaries (female only)

kidney

muscle blocks

spiral valve

first dorsal fin

pelvic fin

liver

gill

pectoral fin

spine

heart

gill slits

eye

mouth

jaw muscles

snout

eye

nostril

barbel

olfactory organ

stomach (out of position to show anatomy)

skeleton made of gristle (cartilage) rather than true bone. They have **gills** (blood-filled structures used to extract oxygen from the water); most sharks have five **gill openings** on each side of the head, although primitive species may have up to seven. Rays only ever have five gill openings. Their skin is covered with small thorny scales called **denticles**, which, when examined in detail, look like small teeth and provide a strong protective coat for the animal. The muscles of the shark's body are segmented into blocks, whereas bony fish have muscles in plate-like sections. This segmented arrangement allows the smooth, undulating swimming movements that are so characteristic of this group.

Sharks come in many shapes, but the familiar form is elongated and streamlined. The fins of the shark are arranged to enhance the balance and position of the animal when swimming in the water. There are four types of fin: the **pectoral fins** are a pair of fins behind or below the gill opening, the **dorsal fin** or fins are on the back, the **pelvic fins** are behind the pectoral fins, and the **anal fin** is behind the anus. The top part of the **tail** is longer than the bottom, which creates lift allowing the shark to stay level when swimming, and to swim with great manoeuvrability. The **keel** is a fleshy ridge, usually just in front of the tail, which is used to stabilise the shark in motion.

By contrast, rays are flattened, bottom-living fish with greatly enlarged pectoral fins that are not distinct from the body and look like **wings**. They swim through the water by flapping their pectoral fins. The combined head, trunk and pectoral fins of a ray are known as the **disc**. Rays also have well-developed **spiracles**, vents or openings behind the eyes, through which sea water is taken in for respiration.

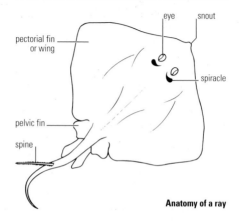

Anatomy of a ray

Sharks and rays have brains that are modified for a highly active life. They also have well-developed sense organs that help them to detect sounds and vibrations and to smell food substances. The sense organs associated with smell (**olfactory organs**) are particularly well developed. Sharks also have a **barbel** under the nose or chin, which is a tentacle-like protuberance or growth used to sense prey by tasting the water. They usually have good eyesight at close range, and some species that live in deep water have particularly large eyes to make the most of the low light conditions. Over the head and down the sides of the body are rows of sensory pores, collectively known as the **lateral** line. This special sensory system helps detect sounds, vibrations and also electrical fields given off by the muscular activity of prey. The signals given out by a wounded and struggling fish attract sharks very quickly. The presence of large quantities of blood in the water may trigger the well-known 'feeding frenzy' when sharks will bite indiscriminately. Some become so frantic they bite each other, and sometimes even themselves!

The body cavity of a shark is often dominated by the **liver**, which in some species is over a third of the body weight. It is rich in oil and serves as a buoyancy mechanism. Rays do not have large livers. The **intestine** is a fairly simple tube, short by fish standards, and the lower portion has a **spiral valve**, which is a fold of intestine that slows down the passage of food and increases the area over which food is absorbed, helping to ensure proper digestion.

The **reproductive organs** of the shark and ray consist of well-developed **ovaries** in females and **testes** in males. Males can easily be identified by the elongated **claspers** adjacent to the pelvic fins. All sharks and rays are fertilised internally, the male introducing sperm into the female using the claspers, resulting in a fertilised egg with a yolk. The shark embryo may develop in egg cases that are laid externally, or the egg case may be shed into the female's **uterus** (reproductive tract) where the embryo stays until birth, or embryos may stay attached directly to the uterus until birth. The young are called **pups** and litter sizes vary between species. In some species, like the Sand Tiger Shark (p. 75), cannibalism occurs within the female (**uterine cannibalism**), one young eating another before they are born.

Sharks and rays are found in almost all seas, and some species even venture into fresh water. From shallow seas to great depths, from tropical to arctic waters they are widely distributed, either as solitary specimens or in vast schools. Many are nocturnal, while others are most active in the twilight hours. Some are highly selective in their choice of food, but others like the Bull Shark (p. 150) will eat almost anything. Their diversity is staggering.

SHARK ATTACK

Despite their reputation, shark attacks on humans are very rare. Fewer than 100 people are attacked worldwide per year, and of these attacks, fewer than 30% prove fatal. Of over 400 species of shark, only 27 have been implicated in attacks on either people or boats, and of these, only four have proven to be a serious risk. The most dangerous species are the Great White Shark (p. 84), the Bull Shark (p. 150), the Oceanic White Tip Shark (p. 152) and the Tiger Shark (p. 163). These species are not only dangerous because of their size, but because they take large prey such as seals. Humans can be and have been mistaken for their natural prey. The Bull Shark is responsible for the majority of attacks on humans mainly because it is widespread, has a curious nature, and lives in inshore waters where humans are most abundant. The Bull Shark has a reputation for eating almost anything, and items such as tin cans, car number plates, nuts and bolts, fish, birds and antelopes as well as human remains have been found in their stomachs.

Much research has been carried out to find effective shark deterrents. Chemicals, fish skin secretions, bubble screen barriers, electric fields and sudden loud noises have all been tried. Some of these are highly specific and will deter certain sharks. However, others have proved useless, and may even attract sharks.

Clearly, the best way to avoid attack is not to swim in the waters known to be frequented by dangerous sharks. These include seal colonies, steep reefs, and areas where there may be industrial discharges of animal wastes, such as around slaughter houses. It is particularly important to leave the water if you are scratched or bleeding, and advisable if very large numbers of potential prey are around, such as fish and squid. In the event of an attack, keeping calm is very important, and attacks have been deterred by people poking the eyes or gills, which are sensitive areas for a shark. Surviving a shark attack depends on quick and appropriate first aid being administered. Treatment for blood loss and shock are critical and medical help should be obtained as soon as possible. Spear fishing is a dangerous activity in shark-infested waters and has resulted in a number of fatalities when sharks have been attracted by wounded and distressed fish, and then attacked the spear fisherman. While many shark attacks have been on skin-divers and surfers, a number of sharks have also been found to be attracted by shiny articles like demand valves on SCUBA diving equipment.

COMMERCIAL EXPLOITATION & CONSERVATION

Sharks and rays are long-lived, top predators that once had few natural enemies, but are now threatened by commercial fishing, sport angling, shark defence nets and the curio trade. They are particularly susceptible to overfishing because their growth is slow, they mature late, and relatively few young are produced each year. Sharks are fished for worldwide, but very few fisheries are properly managed, with the exception of those in temperate waters. Shark flesh is mainly used for human consumption, the fins are believed to be an aphrodisiac, the skin has been used as leather and sand paper, and the jaws and teeth sold as curios and jewellery.

In the tropics, nets to protect bathers on amenity beaches have caught up to 14 species of shark, many of those posing no threat to humans. To stop this needless destruction, net sizes have been increased and nets are being temporarily lifted during 'runs' of prey species.

In the past, shark anglers were no more than trophy hunters. However, in recent years, specimens have been put back alive after photographs are taken, and in some areas individuals are tagged to trace their movements for research purposes. Much research needs to be done on the status and distribution of sharks before adequate measures can be introduced to conserve sharks and rays in our oceans.

SPECIES ENTRIES

Each shark and ray is given its most widely used common name followed by its scientific name in italics. Each entry describes the species' colour, distinctive features, behaviour, depth range and other details. Some sharks are so rare they have only been described from a few specimens and little information is known about them. Others are caught commercially and their importance to man is given.

Size Sharks and rays are measured from the tip of the nose to the tip of the tail (total length). However, some skates and rays are measured across the pectoral fins and this is identified in the text as disc width.

Distribution This summarises the areas where the species has been found. The term circumglobal means a species is found around the globe in a band, normally defined by temperature/latitude.

Food Summarises the main diet; this will vary according to season and prey availability.

Breeding The breeding strategy, gestation period and litter size are given where known.

Danger to humans When a species has been implicated in attacks on humans then this is identified. Those that may cause injury when being handled are also mentioned.

Frilled & Cow Sharks

The frilled and cow sharks (Hexanchiformes) are medium to large sharks (up to 5 m) found throughout the world, mostly in deep water. They are considered to have primitive features and to resemble sharks that are now extinct, having only 1 dorsal fin, and between 6 and 7 gill slits.

There is only one living frilled shark, which has a long, cylindrical, eel-like body designed for hunting prey in caves and crevices. Its mouth is in a forward position and the teeth have 3 points (cusps) in both upper and lower jaws.

Cow sharks have elongated, heavy bodies, a mouth positioned beneath the snout, and comb-like teeth in the lower jaw. The nostrils are not connected to the mouth and there is a distinct notch on the underside of the tip of the tail. This group feeds on a variety of other fish, squid and crab, and is of some commercial importance. Although not normally aggressive, they may bite if provoked.

FRILLED SHARK *Chlamydoselachus anguineus*

An elongated, eel-like shark with 6 pairs of gill slits and a single dorsal fin. The body is dark chocolate-brown, although in some specimens the underside is pale brown. The teeth are small and sharp, and it lives on the sea floor, at depths of between 100 and 1500 m.

Size Males to 1 m; females to 1.4 m.
Distribution A patchy distribution worldwide, preferring deep waters on the outer edge of the continental shelf.
Food Small sharks.
Breeding Live-bearer, with 8–12 young (50 cm) born every 2 years.
Danger to humans Not known to be dangerous.

Frilled Shark

SHARPNOSE SEVENGILL SHARK *Heptranchias perlo*

A strong swimmer with a narrow, pointed head and slender body. The upper surface of the body is brownish-grey, but this fades to pale brown on the underside. The large eyes are useful for hunting on the sea floor at depths to 1000 m, and the jagged teeth help it to grasp slippery prey.

Sharpnose Sevengill Shark

Size Up to 1.3 m.
Distribution Wide-ranging in tropical and temperate seas.
Food Fish and squid.
Breeding Live-bearer, with up to 20 pups per litter.
Danger to humans This shark is aggressive and bites when captured, but is too small to be dangerous.

BLUNTNOSED SIXGILL SHARK *Hexanchus griseus*

This large, heavy-bodied shark is a sluggish swimmer that occurs anywhere from the surface to depths of 2000 m. The colouring varies between pale grey and black-grey to chocolate-brown, fading to grey-white underneath. Most have a pale streak on the lateral line. The comb-shaped teeth are designed to grip a wide variety of slippery prey.

Size Up to 5 m.
Distribution Widely distributed in tropical and temperate seas.
Food Fish, squid, crabs and even seals.
Breeding Litters of over 100 pups have been recorded.
Danger to humans Not known to attack, but can be aggressive if provoked.

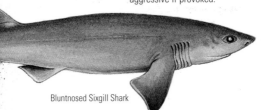

Bluntnosed Sixgill Shark

DOGFISH SHARKS

This large family of sharks (Squaliformes) contains many familiar inshore species as well as rare deep-water giants, reaching up to 8 m in length. Distributed worldwide, this group occupies almost every known oceanic habitat, from shallow water to depths below 10,000 m and from the tropics to arctic regions. Streamlined bodies, pointed snouts, spined dorsal fins and a tail with a knot at the tip and base are characteristic of this group. A number have light-producing organs (photophores) that attract prey and are believed to be used to communicate with others of the same species. Some parasitic dogfish take plugs of flesh from marine mammals and oceanic fish, whereas others have a more varied diet. Dogfish are also a major component in the diet of many other sharks. Some species are solitary, others form huge schools that undergo migrations and are caught commercially. Confirmed attacks on humans are few.

BRAMBLE SHARK *Echinorhinus brucus*

Given its name by the scattered whitish denticles over the body. The body varies between dark purplish-grey and brown, the underside being paler. This large, sluggish shark lives mostly on the sea bed to depths of 1000 m, and only rarely frequents shallow water.

Size Males reach 1.5–2 m; females 2–2.5 m.
Distribution Scattered in tropical and temperate waters mainly in the NE Atlantic and Mediterranean.
Food Smaller sharks, other fish and crabs.
Breeding Live-bearer, with about 20 young per litter.
Danger to humans Not known to be dangerous.

Bramble Shark

Prickly Shark *Echinorhinus cookei*

Named after the small flat denticles covering the body. This shark is grey-brown with a conspicuous white area around the mouth and under the snout. Large, heavy and slow-moving, it lives on the sea floor or in submarine canyons, to depths of 500 m.

Prickly Shark

Size Up to 4 m.
Distribution Scattered throughout the Pacific.
Food A variety of sharks, bony fish, octopus and squid.
Breeding Unknown.
Danger to humans Not known to be dangerous.

GULPER SHARK *Centrophorus granulosus*

Like other gulper sharks, this species has 2 dorsal fins, each with a large spine. This greyish shark lives in water to 1200 m deep. To hunt in this dark environment the Gulper Shark has developed a broad, receptor-covered snout that can detect movement, large eyes to make use of any available light and small teeth to grip prey securely.

Size Up to 1.5 m.
Distribution Scattered throughout the Atlantic, but concentrated in the western Atlantic and Mediterranean. Some records from the Indo-Pacific.
Food Bony fish (hake and lanternfish).
Breeding Live-bearer, litter size not known.
Danger to humans Not dangerous, but should be handled with care as spines are sharp.

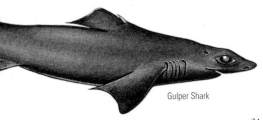

Gulper Shark

LOWFIN GULPER SHARK *Centrophorus lusitanicus*

Lowfin Gulper Shark

This gulper shark has 2 large dorsal fins each with a spine, and a broad, pointed snout. The body is either grey or grey-brown. The large eyes help it to see in low light conditions as it hunts prey over the sea bed at depths of 1500 m. A target species for fishermen in the eastern Atlantic.

Size Up to 1.6 m. Females are slightly larger than males.
Distribution Eastern N Atlantic, western Indian Ocean, S Africa and western Pacific.
Food Fish, squid and crabs.
Breeding Live-bearer, with 6 pups per litter.
Danger to humans Not dangerous, but should be handled with care as spines are sharp.

LEAFSCALE GULPER SHARK *Centrophorus squamosus*

A medium-sized shark with 2 dorsal fins, each with a sharp spine. Recognised by the second fin being set far back on the grey-brown body. The long snout and large eyes are designed for living and hunting in the low light conditions that exist at depths of between 1000 and 2300 m. A fishery exists for Leafscale Gulpers in the eastern Atlantic.

Size Up to 1.5 m. Females are slightly larger than males.
Distribution Widespread in the E Atlantic, Japan, Philippines and New Zealand.
Food No details, but believed to eat fish and squid.
Breeding Live-bearer, with 5 pups per litter.
Danger to humans Not dangerous, but should be handled with care as spines can injure.

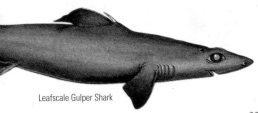

Leafscale Gulper Shark

Little Gulper Shark *Centrophorus uyato*

This grey-brown gulper shark has 2 dorsal fins, each with a small spine on the leading edge. The large eyes and receptors on the slender snout help it to detect prey on or near the sea floor at depths of between 50 and 1500 m. This species is common enough to be a commercial catch in the eastern Atlantic.

Size Up to 1 m.
Distribution Mainly tropical eastern Atlantic, but records exist from other parts of the tropics.
Food Bony fish and squid.
Breeding Live-bearer, giving birth to 1 pup at a time.
Danger to humans Not dangerous, but should be handled with care as spines are sharp.

Little Gulper Shark

BLACK DOGFISH *Centroscyllium fabricii*

A uniformly dark dogfish with 2 dorsal fins, each with a spine on the leading edge. It schools in large numbers on the edge of continental shelves at depths of between 200 and 1600 m, where temperatures range from 1–4°C. In winter months it has been recorded nearer the surface.

Size Up to 1 m.
Distribution Mainly northern Atlantic, but some records from the south-east of Africa.
Food Mostly shellfish, octopus, squid and deep-water bony fish.
Breeding Live-bearer. Litter size not known.
Danger to humans Not dangerous, but should be handled with care as spines are sharp.

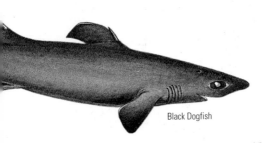

Black Dogfish

COMBTOOTH DOGFISH *Centroscyllium nigrum*

Little is known about this shark. The body is dark with white edges to the dorsal and pectoral fins. Both dorsal fins have spines with grooves. The moderately long snout has receptors to detect prey and the large eyes are needed to see in low light conditions. This species has been caught over the continental slope to depths of 1200 m.

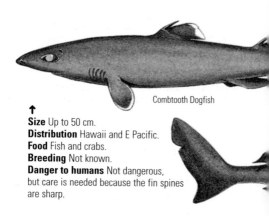

Combtooth Dogfish

↑
Size Up to 50 cm.
Distribution Hawaii and E Pacific.
Food Fish and crabs.
Breeding Not known.
Danger to humans Not dangerous, but care is needed because the fin spines are sharp.

PORTUGUESE DOGFISH *Centroscymnus coelolepis*

A long, stocky dogfish with 2 small dorsal fins and
very small fin spines. This species is both common
and wide-ranging, and is mostly found living near
the sea bed on continental slopes at depths of
between 300 and 4000 m.

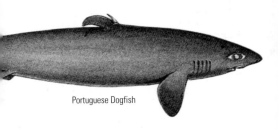

Size Up to 1.2 m.
Distribution NE Atlantic and
Mediterranean, but also recorded from
Newfoundland, Japan, Australia and New
Zealand.
Food Bony fish.
Breeding Live-bearer, with about 15 pups per litter.
Danger to humans Not known to be dangerous.
↓

Portuguese Dogfish

ROUGHSKIN DOGFISH *Centroscymnus owstoni*

A little-known shark that has been recorded at depths of between 500 and 1100 m. It is dark brown or black with 2 dorsal fins and small fin spines that are normally exposed. The teeth in the upper and lower jaws are very different and the lips are thick. The elongated pointed nose and large eyes are characteristic of sharks adapted to life in deep waters as they enable prey to be detected and seen in poor light and murky conditions.

Size Up to 1.2 m.
Distribution Gulf of Mexico, Japan, southern Australia and New Zealand.
Food Presumed to eat bony fish.
Breeding Not known.
Danger to humans Not known to be dangerous. ➡

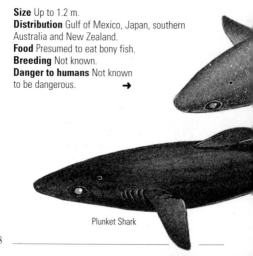

Plunket Shark

PLUNKET SHARK *Centroscymnus plunketi*

This grey-brown dogfish has 2 dorsal fins, each with a short spine, and broad, rounded pectoral fins. Not much is known about this shark except that it occurs in large schools at depths of between 500 and 700 m.

Roughskin Dogfish

Size Males to 1.3 m;
females to 1.7 m.
Distribution SE
Australia and New Zealand.
Food Bony fish and squid.
Breeding Gives birth to as many as 36 pups per litter.
Danger to humans Not known to be dangerous.

29

MANDARIN DOGFISH *Cirrhigaleus barbifer*

This pot-bellied shark has conspicuous flaps of skin over its nostrils under the snout. The fins and tail have pale edges and each of the 2 dorsal fins has a strong spine on the leading edge. Little is known of this shark, but the blade-like cutting teeth and the presence of nasal flaps suggests it locates its prey by sensing chemicals coming from animals living on the sea floor.

Mandarin Dogfish

↑

Size Males to 90 cm; females to 1.2 m.
Distribution Western Pacific, Japan, Australia and New Zealand.
Food Believed to eat bottom-living fish and crabs.
Breeding Live-bearer, with up to 10 embryos found in a single female.
Danger to humans Not known to be dangerous.

DARKIE CHARLIE *Dalatias licha*

This dark, blunt-nosed shark is a versatile predator with large, jagged, triangular teeth in powerful jaws. It is usually found singly over the sea floor, at depths of between 50 and 1800 m. It is also called the Kitefin Shark.

Size Up to 1.8 m. Females are slightly larger than males.
Distribution Most common in the NE Atlantic and Mediterranean, but also found in other parts of tropical and temperate seas.
Food Bony fish, sharks, squid, octopus and shellfish when abundant. Some fast fish have been recorded, suggesting it scavenges or can ambush prey.
Breeding Live-bearer, with litters of 10–16 pups.
Danger to humans Not known to be dangerous.
↓

Darkie Charlie

BIRDBEAK DOGFISH *Deania calcea*

This striking shovel-nosed shark lives on the sea bed on the outer continental slopes at depths to 1500 m. It is dark grey and has 2 dorsal fins, each with grooved spines. The large eyes and small cutting teeth help it to find and grip prey in deep water.

Birdbeak Dogfish

↑

Size Up to 1.1 m. Females are slightly larger than males.
Distribution Scattered throughout tropical and temperate seas; most abundant in the NE Atlantic.
Food Bottom-living bony fish and shellfish.
Breeding Live-bearer, with 6–12 pups per litter.
Danger to humans Not dangerous, but care should be taken when handling owing to spines.

LONGSNOUT DOGFISH *Deania quadrispinosum*

A dark brown dogfish with an extremely long, spade-shaped snout and denticles covering the body. The fins have long upper lobes and short lower lobes, and the notch on the tail fin is conspicuous. Little is known of this shark, but it is found in deep water on the outer continental slopes to depths of 800 m.

Size Up to 1.15 m.
Distribution The southern oceans, southern Australia, New Zealand and S Africa.
Food Bottom-living bony fish.
Breeding Not known.
Danger to humans Care should be taken when handling owing to spines.

↓

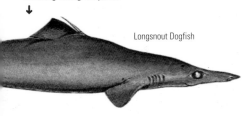

Longsnout Dogfish

BLACKBELLY LANTERNSHARK *Etmopterus lucifer*

A small lanternshark with an elongated, blunt snout. The dorsal fins have spines, the second being larger than the first. There are prominent black markings on the underside of the belly and the eyes are large. This is a wide-ranging species that is found near the sea floor over the continental slope. The name lanternshark comes from the light organs (photophores) over the body.

Blackbelly Lanternshark

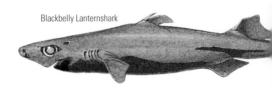

↑
Size Up to 40 cm.
Distribution Mainly throughout the tropical Indo-Pacific and recorded from S America.
Food Small bony fish, squid and crabs.
Breeding Presumed to be a live-bearer.
Danger to humans Too small to be dangerous.

GREAT LANTERNSHARK *Etmopterus princeps*

A dark, squat-bodied lanternshark with 2 spined dorsal fins and large eyes. There are no conspicuous markings, but it does have stout, hooked denticles widely spaced over the body and snout. This species lives over the sea floor at depths of between 500 and 2000 m.

Size Up to 75 cm.
Distribution N Atlantic.
Food Presumably bottom-living fish and squid.
Breeding Not known.
Danger to humans Not known to be dangerous.

↓

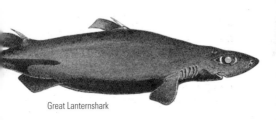

Great Lanternshark

Velvet Belly *Etmopterus spinax*

This small shark is brown above with conspicuous black markings on the underside and 2 dorsal fins with spines. It is common over the continental slope at depths of between 70 and 2000 m. This is also a lanternshark with light organs (photophores) over the body.

Velvet Belly

↑
Size Up to 60 cm.
Distribution Eastern Atlantic and Mediterranean, between Iceland and S Africa.
Food Small bony fish, squid and crabs.
Breeding Live-bearer, with litters of up to 20 pups.
Danger to humans Not known to be dangerous.

GREEN LANTERNSHARK *Etmopterus virens*

This very small, grey-brown lanternshark has black markings on the flanks. The dorsal fins have 2 spines, the second fin being larger than the first. This species is often found in large numbers, which suggests schooling habits and communal hunting. An entire school has been recorded attacking and eating squid that would have been too large for a single individual.

Size Up to 23 cm.
Distribution Gulf of Mexico and Caribbean.
Food Squid.
Breeding Not known.
Danger to humans Too small to be dangerous.

Green Lanternshark

Pygmy Shark *Euprotomicrus bispinatus*

Pygmy Shark

This pygmy shark has large eyes and a round head and snout. The tail is spade-shaped and there are white edges to the fins. Living in mid-water at depths of between 2000 and 10,000 m, this species undergoes extensive vertical migrations to surface waters at night to feed.

Size Up to 27 cm.
Distribution Worldwide, scattered throughout tropical and warm temperate seas.
Food Deep-water bony fish and squid.
Breeding Live-bearer, with 8 young per litter.
Danger to humans Too small to be dangerous.

COOKIECUTTER SHARK *Isistius brasiliensis*

A little, bullet-shaped shark renowned for the large teeth and sucking lips it uses to take plugs of tissue from large fish and whales. It has a prominent dark collar over the gill region, large eyes, a bulbous, short snout and the 2 dorsal fins are set far back on the body. This wide-ranging shark lives at depths of between 100 and 3500 m, and migrates to the surface at night to feed. It has been recorded to bite the rubber sonar domes of nuclear submarines.

Size Up to 50 cm.
Distribution Worldwide, scattered throughout tropical and warm temperate seas.
Food Attacks large bony fish, dolphins and whales, and even the Megamouth Shark (p.78), leaving crater wounds on its victims.
Breeding Not known.
Danger to humans Unlikely to attack bathers owing to habitat preferences, but still a remote possibility.

Cookiecutter Shark

KNIFETOOTH DOGFISH *Scymnodon ringens*

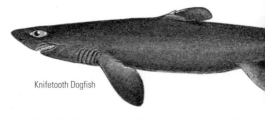

Knifetooth Dogfish

This blackish shark has large cutting teeth in the lower jaw and small spiked ones in the upper, which suggests it is capable of attacking and devouring large prey. The head is thick and high and the snout is broad and short. Little is known about this species except that it is found at depths of between 200 and 1600 m and is surprisingly common at these depths.

Size Up to 1.1 m.
Distribution Eastern Atlantic.
Food Mid-water bony fish.
Breeding Probably a live-bearer.
Danger to humans Not known to be dangerous.

GREENLAND SHARK *Somniosus microcephalus*

A very large, sluggish, heavy-bodied shark that shows no resistance when caught. The snout is short and rounded and the dorsal fins are relatively small and spineless. An abundant species in shallow estuaries during colder months, it moves to deeper water as the temperature increases. It lives on the sea floor, to depths of 1200 m.

Size Males to 3.5 m; females to 7.5 m.
Distribution Northern Atlantic and Arctic, but some records from the southern oceans.
Food Although slow-moving it can capture large and active bony fish, seals and small whales. It also feeds on carrion and offal from whaling stations.
Breeding Live-bearer, with up to 10 young per litter.
Danger to humans No substantiated records of attacks on humans.

Greenland Shark

PACIFIC SLEEPER SHARK *Somniosus pacificus*

A stout, sluggish shark with small dorsal fins without spines, and small eyes. It is normally mid-grey, but some specimens are black. A common species in temperate waters on the northern Pacific continental slopes where it ranges between the shore and depths of 2000 m.

Pacific Sleeper Shark

Size Estimated to reach 7 m from deep-water photographs.
Distribution Northern Pacific, although there are some records from the southern seas.
Food Fish, seals, octopus and bottom-living shellfish.
Breeding Live-bearer, with some adult females recorded with up to 300 eggs inside.
Danger to humans Not known to be dangerous.

Spined Pygmy Shark *Squaliolus laticaudus*

The smallest shark in the world and the only one with a single spine on the first dorsal fin and none on the second. The tail is spade-shaped and there are pale edges to the fins, and it has well-developed light-emitting organs (photophores) on the underside of the body, which enable individuals to locate one another. It is a wide-ranging species over continental slopes (to depths of 500 m) and it migrates to the surface at night to feed.

Size Up to 25 cm, matures at 15–17 cm.
Distribution Worldwide in tropical and temperate seas.
Food Deep-water squid and bony fish.
Breeding Probably a live-bearer, with up to 12 mature eggs found in a single female.
Danger to humans Not known to be dangerous.

Spined Pygmy Shark

SPURDOG *Squalus acanthias*

This is the most important commercial shark. It has
2 spined dorsal fins and white spots on a grey body.
This extremely abundant dogfish occupies inshore
waters where large schools pursue and feed upon
mid-water fish. It is recorded to depths of
900 m, undergoing seasonal migrations to keep
within a 7–15°C temperature band. It is known to
live up to 30 years, with some estimating its life span
to be 70 years. It is also called the Piked Dogfish,
Spiny Dogfish and the Victorian Spotted Dogfish.

Size Males to 1 m; females to 1.65 m.
Distribution Circumglobal in temperate zone.

Food A voracious predator feeding on mid-water and bottom-living bony fish, squid and shellfish.
Breeding Mates in winter, gestation lasting between 18 and 24 months. It gives birth to up to 20 live young per litter.
Danger to humans Care needed when handling as spines are sharp.

Spurdog

SHORTNOSE SPURDOG *Squalus megalops*

This small dogfish has 2 dorsal fins, each with a spine. The body is grey-brown above, lighter below, and has no spots. The fins have white edges and the front of the dorsal fin has a conspicuous black rim. This species is common in large schools to depths of 700 m.

Size Up to 71 cm.
Distribution Mainly S Australia but possible records from southern Africa and the western Pacific.

Shortnose Spurdog

Food A variety of small mid-water and bottom-living bony fish, other sharks, crabs and squid.
Breeding Live-bearer, with litters of about 3 pups born between October and December.
Danger to humans Care needed when handling as spines are sharp.

SHORTSPINE SPURDOG *Squalus mitsukurii*

A small, dark spurdog with spines on both dorsal fins. The first dorsal fin is high, and there are conspicuous keels (projections) on both sides of the tail. Caught commercially over the continental shelf in the northern Pacific, to depths of 750 m.

Size Up to 1.1 m.
Distribution Circumglobal in tropical and warm temperate waters.
Food Bony fish, crabs and octopus.
Breeding Gestation may last up to 2 years. Live-bearer, with up to 9 pups usually born in the autumn.
Danger to humans Care needed when handling as spines are sharp.

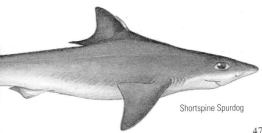

Shortspine Spurdog

PRICKLY DOGFISH *Oxynotus bruniensis*

A small, stout dogfish with high, sail-like dorsal fins and a large tail. The spines on the dorsal fins are small and the body is a uniform grey-brown colour. Not much is known about this shark, but it is fairly common, living over the sea floor of the continental shelf at depths to 500 m.

Prickly Dogfish

↑
Size Up to 72 cm.
Distribution
Southern Australia
and New Zealand.
Food Not known.
Breeding Live-bearer,
with up to 7 embryos
recorded from 1 female.
Danger to humans Not
known to be dangerous.

ANGULAR ROUGH SHARK *Oyxnotus centrina*

A rough shark with conspicuous sail-like dorsal
fins, a blunt snout and a squat body. The body is
grey-brown, with light horizontal lines on the
head. Little is known about this bottom-living
shark.

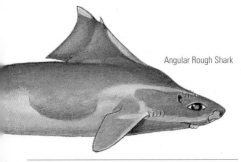

Size Up to 1.5 m.
Distribution Temperate NE Atlantic and
Mediterranean.
Food Recorded as eating bristle worms and
probably eats bottom-living fish.
Breeding Live-bearer, with up to 8 pups per litter.
Danger to humans Not known to be dangerous.
↓

Angular Rough Shark

SAWSHARKS

Sawsharks (Pristiophoriformes) may grow up to 2 m in length and are found in the Indo-Pacific and Caribbean on the continental shelf and upper slopes in temperate and tropical seas. As their name suggests, they have a long snout with pairs of projecting teeth that resemble a saw. The body is elongated with 2 dorsal fins without spines and there is no anal fin. The long, paired barbels are positioned under the snout and the 5 or 6 pairs of gill slits are situated on the side of the head. They feed on fish, crabs and squid and are believed to use the 'saw' to damage and kill their prey and to dislodge prey from the sea bed. Sawsharks are caught commercially and used for human consumption. They are not known to be dangerous, but the teeth are sharp and these sharks should be handled with care.

SIXGILL SAWSHARK *Pliotrema warreni*

This sawshark has an unmistakable snout, with saw teeth and 2 long barbels on a long and flattened body. The barbels are used as sensors to detect food and the snout dislodges prey buried in sand. It is commonly found on the sea bed, in large schools, at depths to 430 m.

Size Up to 1.4 m.
Distribution Western Indian Ocean, Cape Coast to Mozambique.

Food Mainly feeds on bottom-living fish, crabs and squid.

Breeding Live-bearer, with litters of up to 17 young.

Danger to humans Not dangerous.

Sixgill Sawshark

LONGNOSE SAWSHARK *Pristiophorus cirratus*

The body of this sawshark is grey-brown with some darker markings and spots. It has the characteristic long snout with lateral teeth. The 2 barbels are used to detect prey on the sandy floors of bays and estuaries, and offshore to depths of 300 m where it feeds in schools. This sawshark is an important commercial species.

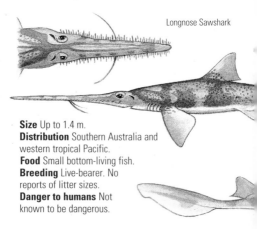

Longnose Sawshark

Size Up to 1.4 m.
Distribution Southern Australia and western tropical Pacific.
Food Small bottom-living fish.
Breeding Live-bearer. No reports of litter sizes.
Danger to humans Not known to be dangerous.

JAPANESE SAWSHARK *Pristiophorus japonicus*

A grey-brown sawshark with the familiar flattened head and body, narrow snout and lateral teeth. Prey is detected with the 2 barbels and dislodged from the sea bed with the long snout. It is commonly caught over sand and mud in coastal waters and eaten in Japan as 'kameboko'.

Size Up to 1.4 m.
Distribution NW Pacific.
Food Bottom-living fish and shellfish.
Breeding Live-bearer, with up to 12 young per litter.
Danger to humans Not known to be dangerous.

↓

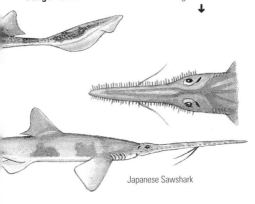

Japanese Sawshark

BULLHEAD SHARKS

Bullhead or horn sharks (Heterodontiformes) are medium-sized (up to 1.6 m), and restricted to tropical and warm temperate seas, usually in shallow water. They have large, blunt heads with a crest above each eye. The paired fins are relatively large and paddle-like and these are the only sharks with dorsal fins that have spines, and an anal fin. The mouth is sited at the front of the head and is connected to the nostrils by a groove. They are slow swimmers, active at night and eat a variety of bottom-living organisms. They are not a target species for commercial fishermen, but are caught in bottom trawls when they are used for human consumption and fishmeal. They are not dangerous to humans, but will bite if harassed.

CRESTED BULLHEAD SHARK *Heterodontus galeatus*

A sluggish bullhead shark with characteristic grey-brown colour, broad, dark saddle markings on the head and body and prominent spined dorsal fins. The snout is blunt with a high forehead and the fins are paddle-like. It is common on sea floors, usually close inshore, where it occupies rocky crevices during the day and emerges to hunt at night.

Size Up to 1.5 m.
Distribution East coast of Australia.
Food Sea urchins, crabs, sea snails and small fish.
Breeding Egg cases are laid at depths of 20–30 m among seaweed and sponges; these hatch 8 months later.
Danger to humans Not known to be dangerous.

Crested Bullhead Shark

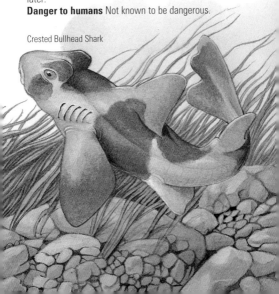

PORT JACKSON SHARK *Heterodontus portusjacksoni*

This distinctive bullhead shark has a large blunt head, large spined dorsal fins and a grey body with a conspicuous black harness on the back and flanks. A common, inshore shark living in caves with sandy floors. It is territorial and undergoes short seasonal migrations.

Port Jackson Shark

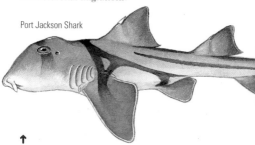

↑

Size Up to 1.65 m.
Females are larger than males.
Distribution Southern Australia.
Food Prey items include sea urchins, starfish, bottom-living invertebrates and occasionally garbage: mammal fur, orange and potato peelings have all been found in specimens!
Breeding Live-bearer. They favour certain communal breeding sites.
Danger to humans Considered harmless, but bites if provoked.

ZEBRA BULLHEAD SHARK *Heterodontus zebra*

Striking zebra stripes run the length of the body of this small bullhead shark. It has 2 dorsal fins, each with a spine. This species is commonly found living over the sea floor in inshore waters where it crawls and swims slowly over rock, seaweed and sand. Despite it being a common species, little is known about it.

Size Up to 1.2 m.
Distribution Northern Australia and western Pacific.
Food Probably eats bottom-living invertebrates.
Breeding Live-bearer. Litter size not known.
Danger to humans Bites if provoked.

Zebra Bullhead Shark

57

CARPET SHARKS

The carpet sharks (Orectolobiformes) make up a diverse group that includes the largest living fish, the Whale Shark(p.72), which can reach a length of 18 m. Carpet sharks are mostly found in temperate and tropical seas. They have flattened bodies and virtually all live on the sea floor. Carpet sharks feed on a variety of bottom-living fish and invertebrates. Many in this group feature in commercial catches. The majority of carpet sharks are too small to be dangerous, but many will bite if provoked.

NECKLACE CARPET SHARK *Parascyllium variolatum*

A small, strikingly-marked carpet shark recognised by a dark, white-spotted collar around the gills, a white-spotted body and black marks on the fins. Little is known about this bottom-living species except that it is nocturnal and found in beds of algae and sea grass near rocky reefs.

Size Up to 90 cm.
Distribution S and western Australia.
Food Unknown.
Breeding Live-bearer.
Danger to humans Not known to be dangerous.

Necklace Carpet Shark

BLIND SHARK *Brachaelurus waddi*

A small, stout shark with barbels extending in front of a short mouth and very large spiracles behind the eyes. Two large, spineless dorsal fins are positioned towards the rear of the body. The body is black to light brown, sometimes with small white spots. It is common inshore over rocky shores and reefs to depths of about 100 m.

Blind Shark

↑
Size Up to 1.2 m.
Distribution Eastern Australia.
Food Crabs, shrimp, cuttlefish and small fish.
Breeding Live-bearer, with up to 8 young per litter.
Danger to humans Not known to be dangerous.

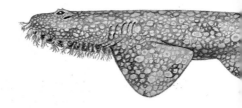

TASSELLED WOBBEGONG *Eucrossorhinus dasypogon*

A large, squat shark recognised by fleshy tassels fringing the head. It is grey to yellowish-brown and highly patterned. The fins are wide, with the dorsal ones set well back on the body. A solitary fish, found in or near coral reefs, resting in caves during the day and feeding at night.

Size Up to 3.6 m.
Distribution Northern Australia and Papua New Guinea.
Food Bottom-living invertebrates and fish, including squirrelfish and soldierfish.
Breeding Probably live-bearer. Numbers not known.
Danger to humans Possibly the most aggressive of the wobbegongs and responsible for several unprovoked attacks. Recorded to have attacked and killed local people in Papua New Guinea.

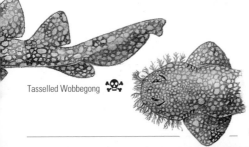

Tasselled Wobbegong

JAPANESE WOBBEGONG *Orectolobus japonicus*

A small wobbegong with a highly decorative pattern of spots and lines and 5 or 6 fleshy growths under the eyes. The nasal barbels are sensitive feelers that can detect prey buried in sand. A nocturnal species, living over the sea floor, it is known to migrate inshore to mate and give birth.

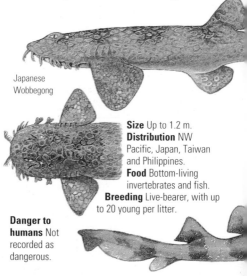

Japanese Wobbegong

Size Up to 1.2 m.
Distribution NW Pacific, Japan, Taiwan and Philippines.
Food Bottom-living invertebrates and fish.
Breeding Live-bearer, with up to 20 young per litter.

Danger to humans Not recorded as dangerous.

SPOTTED WOBBEGONG *Orectolobus maculatus*

A large, solid wobbegong with only a few lobes on the edge of the head. The handsomely patterned body is pale brown and greenish, with pale spots defined by white edges. Although sluggish during the day, this shark is active at night when it stalks its prey. An abundant species found from the shore to depths of 110 m where fishermen find them wedged in lobster pots.

Size Up to 3.2 m.

Distribution Around Australia and possibly as far north as Japan.

Food Bottom-living invertebrates and bony fish.

Breeding Live-bearer, with up to 37 young per litter.

Danger to humans An aggressive shark with records of unprovoked attacks on divers and boats, characteristically holding on after biting.

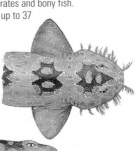

Spotted Wobbegong

COBBLER WOBBEGONG *Sutorectus tentaculatus*

A relatively slim, patterned wobbegong with characteristic rows of warty growths over the head and down the body. It is pale brown with dark brown saddles and blotches. The 2 large dorsal fins are placed towards the rear of the body. It occupies inshore rocky and coral reefs, but little else is known of its biology.

Size Up to 1 m (but unconfirmed reports of 3 m).
Distribution Southern and western Australia.
Food Bottom-living invertebrates and fish.
Breeding Live-bearer. Numbers not known.
Danger to humans Likely to bite if provoked.
↓

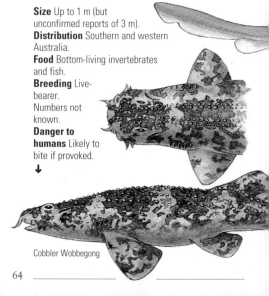

Cobbler Wobbegong

Grey Bamboo Shark *Chiloscyllium griseum*

This bamboo shark has 2 spineless dorsal fins, and an anal fin close to the tail. The young have dark brown bands on the body and head, whereas the adults are uniform grey or pale brown. This species is common in inshore waters and typically lives deep in crevices.

Grey Bamboo Shark

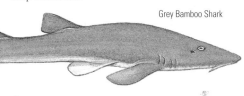

↑

Size Up to 75 cm.
Distribution Northern Indian Ocean, between the Gulf of Iran and Japan.
Food Mainly bottom-living invertebrates.
Breeding Lays eggs in small, oval egg cases on reefs.
Danger to humans May bite if harassed.

SLENDER BAMBOO SHARK *Chiloscyllium indicum*

An elongated shark with a characteristic dark brown spotted pattern on the body and fins. It has 2 dorsal fins and an anal fin joining the tail. All the fins are thin, and not at all muscular. A common inshore species living on the sea floor, but little is known of its biology.

Slender Bamboo Shark

Size Up to 65 cm.
Distribution Northern Indian Ocean, between the Arabian Gulf and Japan.
Food Bottom-living invertebrates.
Breeding Live-bearer. Numbers not known.
Danger to humans Not known to be dangerous.

BROWN BANDED BAMBOO SHARK *Chiloscyllium punctatum*

A small, slender shark with a short, rounded snout, large dorsal fins and barbels on the chin. The body is usually brown, but may be banded in some individuals. Young sharks are patterned with saddles and a few scattered dark spots. A common inshore species, found on coral reefs and often in rock pools as it can survive out of water for several hours.

Size Up to 1.04 m.
Distribution Northern Indian Ocean, western Pacific and northern Australia.
Food Bottom-living invertebrates.
Breeding Lays rounded eggs. Numbers not known.
Danger to humans May bite if provoked.

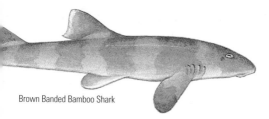

Brown Banded Bamboo Shark

SPECKLED CARPET SHARK *Hemiscyllium trispeculare*

Speckled Carpet Shark

A slender shark with dark brown spots over the body and a conspicuous large black spot behind the gills. The mouth is placed well forward and the tail is elongated. This is a common coral reef-dwelling shark, which is often found in rock pools.

Size Up to 64 cm.
Distribution Northern Australia.
Food Mainly bottom-living invertebrates.
Breeding Live-bearer.
Danger to humans Not known to be dangerous.

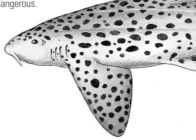

ZEBRA SHARK *Stegostoma fasciatum*

A large, unmistakable shark with big, dark brown spots on a yellowish or brown body. The blade-like tail is almost half the length of the body. It has a blunt head and the nasal barbels are conspicuous. This sluggish species is often found resting on sandy reef areas, but it enters caves and crevices, using its long flexible body, to look for prey.

Size Up to 3.5 m.
Distribution Red Sea, Indian Ocean, western Pacific and northern Australia.
Food Bottom-living snails, crabs and small bony fish.

Zebra Shark

Breeding Lays large brown or purplish egg cases with lateral tufts that anchor them to objects or rocks.
Danger to humans Unaggressive, no recorded attacks on people.

NURSE SHARK *Ginglymostoma cirratum*

A large, heavy-bodied, yellow-brown to grey-brown shark that is sluggish during the day, but active at night. This species lives in shallow coastal waters, and is often found in defined resting sites, in schools of up to 30 individuals. Commonly used in behavioural and physiological research, this species is also regularly kept in large aquaria.

Nurse Shark

↑

Size Up to 4.3 m.
Distribution Tropical and warm temperate Atlantic and eastern Pacific.
Food Bottom-living invertebrates, and fish, including stingrays.
Breeding Complicated courtship with parallel swimming and male biting female in copulation. Live-bearer, with up to 25 young per litter.
Danger to humans Mainly non-aggressive, although may bite with a powerful vice-like grip if provoked.

Tawny Nurse Shark *Nebrius ferrugineus*

This large, sluggish, brown nurse shark is reported by anglers to be a powerful fighter. It is commonly found near coral and rocky reefs where it shelters in daytime and hunts at night. They are social sharks that rest in groups of 2 to 12 and are often seen piled motionless on top of one another.

Size Up to 3.2 m.
Distribution Tropical Indian Ocean, northern Australia and central Pacific.
Food Bottom-living invertebrates and reef fish.
Breeding Live-bearer, with up to 8 young per litter.
Danger to humans Generally docile, allowing humans to play with it, but is capable of a dangerous bite and should be treated with respect.

Tawny Nurse Shark

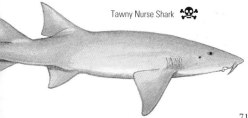

WHALE SHARK *Rhiniodon typus*

This is the world's largest fish. An unmistakable creature with a large, rectangular mouth, small eyes and huge gill slits. The enormous body has ridges running down the sides, and is covered with white spots. This mid-water, oceanic shark is usually solitary, but may be seen in groups of over 100 individuals. It migrates, timing its movements with changes in sea temperature and availability of plankton, on which it feeds.

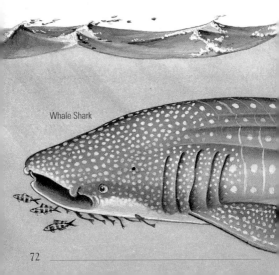

Whale Shark

Size Possibly up to 18 m, but over 12 m is rare.
Distribution Circumglobal in tropical and warm
temperate seas.
Food Filter-feeds on plankton and occasionally eats
other fish.
Breeding Live-bearer. Recently 300 embryos were
found in a female 10.5 m long.
Danger to humans Considered harmless with no
evidence of aggression to divers who may even ride on
backs or fins. However, there are some
reports of this shark butting fishing boats.

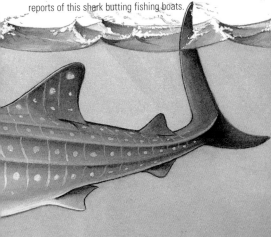

MACKEREL SHARKS

This group (Lamniformes) contains some very large sharks; as adults none are smaller than 1 m and most reach 3 m or more. Mackerel sharks are distributed in tropical and temperate seas. The majority are built for speed with cylindrical bodies and a large, powerful tail. They feed on bony fish and mammals, although 2 species filter-feed on plankton. Some in this group are commercially important owing to the high-quality meat. Mackerel sharks, which include the Great White Shark (p.84), are known to attack humans.

SAND TIGER SHARK *Eugomphodus taurus* ☠️

A large, heavy-bodied shark with a mouth containing conspicuous teeth giving it the alternative name of Snaggle-tooth Shark. The body is mostly pale brown, but spotted individuals have been recorded. This species is common singly, or in large schools, in inshore waters over coral and rocky reefs where it is most active at night.

Size Up to 3 m.
Distribution Found in warm temperate and tropical waters except west coast of America.

Food A voracious feeder on many species of bony fish, other sharks, squid and shellfish.

Breeding Up to 23 eggs are produced in each female, but the dominant pup, which has functional teeth at 17 cm, eats the others before it is born (uterine cannibalism) and hatches after 9 months at 1 m long.

Danger to humans Has a bad reputation in Australian waters but is probably confused with other sharks.

Sand Tiger Shark

SMALLTOOTH SAND TIGER *Odontaspis ferox*

A large, bulky shark with a long, conical nose, large eyes and a conspicuous mouth. It has prominent teeth and a large front dorsal fin. The body is grey, sometimes with reddish blotches. This shark is found near the sea floor over continental slopes to depths of 420 m.

Smalltooth Sand Tiger

Size Up to 3.6 m.
Distribution
Circumglobal in warm temperate and tropical waters.
Food Bony fish, squid and bottom-living crabs.
Breeding Unknown, presumed similar to the Sand Tiger (p. 74).
Danger to humans Rarely encountered and no records of aggression.

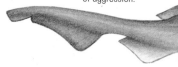

GOBLIN SHARK *Mitsukurina owstoni*

The most extraordinary of all the sharks. It is large, pale and pinkish with an unusual head and a greatly elongated, flattened snout. The teeth are long and pointed, set in highly extendible jaws. Some of the gill filaments are exposed, and the body is soft with a long tail fin. An uncommon, slow, bottom-living species mostly occupying deep water at depths of about 500 m. Sensors in the blade-like snout may be used to detect the electrical fields generated by the muscle activity of prey.

Size Up to 3.3 m.
Distribution Warm temperate seas throughout the world.
Food Fish, squid and crabs.
Breeding Unknown.
Danger to humans Believed to be harmless.

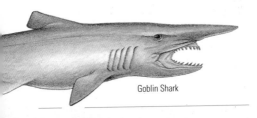

Goblin Shark

MEGAMOUTH SHARK *Megachasma pelagios*

A recently discovered, huge, filter-feeding shark,
with a blubbery head and front-projecting
mouth. The body is soft and flabby, the pectoral fins are
long and the tail is strong. The gill openings are
small, suggesting an inactive shark. It is
possibly wide-ranging at depths of between
100 and 1000 m and moves nearer the
surface at night following its prey.
This species is the only known
shark victim of the Cookiecutter Shark (p. 39) owing
to its soft skin and mid-
water habit. The latest

record is the first female ever recorded, which was found stranded in Japan. The Megamouth Shark is likely to remain a rare catch due to its feeding habits and preferred habitat.

Size Up to 5.5 m.
Distribution Pacific, off Hawaii, Japan, southern California and western Australia.
Food Filter-feeds on small shrimps, shellfish and jellyfish.
Breeding Unknown.
Danger to humans Few live encounters with this shark. Not thought to be dangerous.

Megamouth Shark

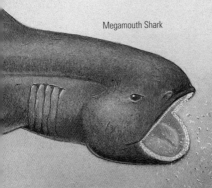

Bigeye Thresher *Alopias superciliosus*

A very large, greyish-brown thresher shark with a dorsal tail fin nearly equal in length to the rest of the body. The eyes are huge, directed forwards and upwards, and the head has grooves on top. It is common in coastal waters, occasionally to depths of 500 m. A strong swimmer, it is reported to circle schools of fish which it stuns or kills with thrashes of the tail fin.

Bigeye Thresher

Size Up to 4.5 m.
Distribution Circumglobal in tropical and warm temperate waters.
Food Mainly fish, including herring, mackerel and squid.
Breeding Live-bearer with up to 4 per litter; the others are eaten before they are born by the dominant pup (uterine cannibalism).
Danger to humans Potentially as dangerous as other thresher sharks (p. 81).

THRESHER SHARK *Alopias vulpinus*

A very large thresher shark with a greatly elongated tail, equal in length to the body. The dorsal fin is high and the pectoral fins are large. There are white markings on the abdomen and the teeth are small and pointed. A coastal species, found from the surface to depths of about 350 m. A strong swimmer, which herds and stuns prey with the long tail fin.

Size Up to 6 m.
Distribution Circumglobal in temperate and tropical oceans.
Food Mostly schooling fish, squid and shellfish and sometimes sea birds.
Breeding Live-bearer, usually producing 2 young per litter; the others are eaten before they are born by the dominant pups (uterine cannibalism).
Danger to humans Recorded attacks on boats, unconfirmed anecdote of fisherman decapitated by a stroke of the tail.

Thresher Shark

BASKING SHARK *Cetorhinus maximus*

Mostly seen from prominent headlands when on migration. This huge, grey shark occurs either singly or in large schools and is most conspicuous when feeding on the surface, when the snout, dorsal fin and tail are all visible above the water line. Below, the minute teeth and modified gills provide a filtering screen for its prey, plankton. It has been recorded jumping from water (breaching) to remove parasites from the body.

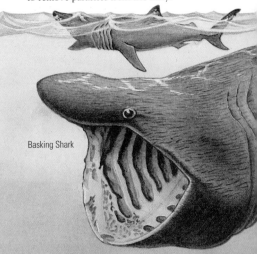

Basking Shark

Size Up to 15 m, but rarely exceeds 10 m.
Distribution Global, oceanic in cool and temperate seas, avoids tropics.
Food Planktonic shellfish and invertebrates. An average adult filters 2000 tonnes of water per hour and the stomach may contain half a tonne of plankton.
Breeding Live-bearers; the large numbers of eggs suggests that dominant pups feed on the others before they are born (uterine cannibalism).
Danger to humans Generally harmless, but huge size should be respected.

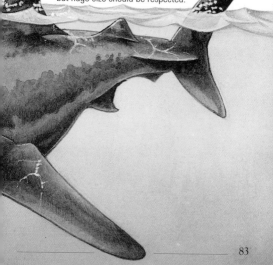

GREAT WHITE SHARK *Carcharodon carcharias* ☠☠ ☠☠

The famous Great White or White Pointer is a huge, heavy-bodied shark with a crescent-shaped tail fin, and large, triangular, jagged teeth. This is mainly a coastal species found between the surface and depths of 1280 m, often associated with seal colonies. This shark was an important big game fish, but it is now protected in certain areas as over-fishing has reduced its numbers.

Great White Shark
☠☠ ☠☠

Size Up to 8 m.
Distribution Circumglobal in tropical and temperate seas. Less common in the tropics.
Food A super-predator, which readily scavenges as well as preying on bony fish and other sharks, sea turtles, sea birds and marine mammals, including porpoises, dolphins, seals and sea otters.
Breeding Live-bearer, with suspected uterine cannibalism and up to 9 young per litter.

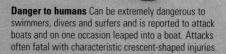

Danger to humans Can be extremely dangerous to swimmers, divers and surfers and is reported to attack boats and on one occasion leaped into a boat. Attacks often fatal with characteristic crescent-shaped injuries.

SHORTFIN MAKO *Isurus oxyrinchus* ☠

The Shortfin Mako is the fastest recorded shark, capable of jumping from the water (breaching). It is an important big game fish. The body is large, streamlined and deep cobalt-blue with a white underside. It is an oceanic fish living between the surface and depths of 150 m and is known to undergo extensive migrations northwards in the summer months following the warm water. An important long-line fishery revolves around this species owing to the high quality of its meat.

Shortfin Mako
☠

Size Possibly up to 4 m.
Distribution Circumglobal in tropical and temperate waters.
Food Mainly mid-water schooling bony fish although occasionally other sharks, turtles, porpoises and squid.
Breeding Live-bearer, with up to 16 pups per litter.
Danger to humans Some recorded attacks on swimmers, divers and boats, but occurs too far offshore for frequent contact.

PORBEAGLE *Lamna nasus*

This common, mid-water shark is blue-grey fading to white on the underside. It occurs singly or in schools, preferring water at less than 18°C. The large, heavy body is streamlined and the teeth are large and blade-like. It is caught at depths to 360 m and significant long-line fisheries exist for this species.

Size Up to 3.7 m.
Distribution Temperate and cooler waters as far north as Iceland.
Food Schooling fish, including other sharks.
Breeding Probably live-bearing, with up to 5 pups that feed on fertilised eggs before birth (uterine cannibalism).
Danger to humans Potentially dangerous, but seldom confirmed in attacks; probably confused with the Great White Shark (p.84).

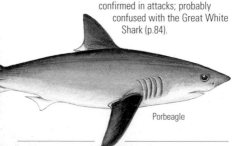

Porbeagle

Ground Sharks

An enormous group of sharks (Carchariniformes), the largest reaching up to 6 m. Ground sharks are distributed around the world in temperate and tropical waters. Characterised by a cylindrical body and a conical head, they feed on schooling bony fish, squid and invertebrates. This group contains some of the most commercially important species. Most are harmless unless provoked; however, some in this group are responsible for the majority of attacks on humans. The most dangerous is the Bull Shark (p. 150).

Brown Catshark *Apristurus brunneus*

This small catshark is uniformly dark brown with conspicuous pale edges to the fins and a humped body. Little is known about this bottom-living species, although it has been found in deep water over the continental shelf to depths of 950 m.

Size Up to 68 cm.
Distribution Tropical and temperate eastern Pacific.
Food Mainly shrimps and squid.
Breeding One egg is laid at a time; each is 5 cm long with long tendrils and takes about 1 year to hatch.
Danger to humans Not known to be dangerous.

Brown Catshark

MADEIRA CATSHARK *Apristurus maderensis*

A slender-bodied shark, with a broad, flattened snout and large eyes. There are no conspicuous markings, and the black body is smooth. The small dorsal fins are set far back on the body. It lives on the sea floor, on continental slopes at depths of between 700 and 1500 m.

Madeira Catshark

↑
Size Up to 68 cm.
Distribution NE Atlantic and Madeira, possibly as far north as Iceland.
Food No information, but presumably bottom-living shellfish.
Breeding Produces a single egg.
Danger to humans Not known to be dangerous.

AUSTRALIAN SPOTTED CATSHARK *Asymbolus analis*

A small, elongated catshark with scattered rusty spots and light brown saddle markings on the flanks. The snout is short and rounded and the teeth are small. Males have pelvic fins that are joined, forming a skin flap around the claspers. It is found off coasts in temperate waters, where it lives on the sea floor.

Size Up to 60 cm.
Distribution South-eastern Australia.
Food Little known, but probably bottom-living invertebrates.
Breeding Live-bearer, but little else is known.
Danger to humans Not known to be dangerous.
↓

Australian Spotted Catshark

GULF CATSHARK *Asymbolus vincenti*

A small catshark with a short, rounded snout and a
dark, chocolate-brown body covered in numerous
scattered white spots. This bottom-living, coastal
species is found at depths to 220 m.

Gulf Catshark

↑

Size Up to 60 cm.
Distribution Southern Australia.
Food Not known, but probably bottom-living
invertebrates.
Breeding Lays 1 egg at a time. The egg case is 5 cm
long with long tendrils.
**Danger to
humans** Not
known to be
dangerous.

Australian Marbled Catshark *Atelomycterus macleayi*

A slender, narrow-headed catshark with highly variable colouring. The saddle markings on its back are on a pale background covered with numerous scattered black spots. Little is known of this catshark except that it is found over sand and rock in shallow water.

Size Up to 60 cm.
Distribution Tropical north-western Australia.
Food Not known, but presumably bottom-living invertebrates.
Breeding Lays eggs.
Danger to humans Not known to be dangerous.

Australian Marbled Catshark

CORAL CATSHARK *Atelomycterus marmoratus*

A small, slender catshark with a narrow head and variable colour patterns. This is a well-known inshore species found associated with coral reefs, hence the common name.

Coral Catshark

Size Up to 70 cm.
Distribution Northern Indian Ocean between Pakistan and New Guinea and the South China sea.
Food Probably reef invertebrates and small fish.
Breeding Lays 1 egg at a time.
Danger to humans Not known to be dangerous.

BLACKSPOTTED CATSHARK *Aulohalaelurus labiosus*

This coastal, bottom-living catshark is most active at night. It has a cylindrical, elongated body with dusky saddle markings, the skin being firm and thick. The 2 dorsal fins are of equal size and the eyes are small. Little is known about this shark.

Size Up to 67 cm.
Distribution South-western Australia.
Food Not known, but probably bottom-living invertebrates.
Breeding Probably lays eggs.
Danger to humans Not known to be dangerous.

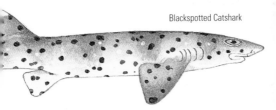

Blackspotted Catshark

95

AUSTRALIAN SWELLSHARK *Cephaloscyllium laticeps*

This species is called a swellshark because it can inflate itself with air or water. It has a stout body and highly variable colouring. It is usually found inshore, but has been recorded to depths of 220 m. Fishermen consider this species a nuisance because it takes lobsters from fishing pots.

Australian Swellshark

↑
Size Up to 1.5 m, but rarely over 1 m.
Distribution Southern Australia.
Food Preys on small fish, shellfish and squid.
Breeding Lays eggs with characteristic ridged cases.
Danger to humans Not known to be dangerous.

SWELLSHARK *Cephaloscyllium ventriosum*

When harassed, this lightly patterned shark can inflate itself like a pufferfish, hence its name. It is a sluggish mover, preferring rocky, seaweed-covered areas in shallow water, although it has been recorded to depths of 450 m. It is nocturnal, and may occur in groups, when individuals pile on top of one another, forming a heap.

Size Up to 1 m.
Distribution Eastern Pacific.
Food Bottom-living fish and shellfish.
Breeding Lays eggs with large amber-green cases. They hatch after 10 months.
Danger to humans Harmless to people, but may bite if harassed.

Swellshark

ROUGHTAIL CATSHARK *Galeus arae*

This very small catshark has a long, compressed snout and 2 small dorsal fins. The body is covered in blotches and there are saddle markings on the flanks. This shark lives over the sea floor and is sometimes found in dense groups. Although it has been recorded as deep as 730 m, it rarely goes below 140 m.

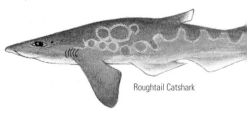

Roughtail Catshark

Size Up to 45 cm.
Distribution Caribbean.
Food Mainly deep-water shrimps.
Breeding May lay eggs or give birth to live young.
Danger to humans Not known to be dangerous.

AUSTRALIAN SAWTAIL CATSHARK *Galeus boardmani*

Little is known about this small, colourful shark. This is surprising as the saddle markings outlined with white, the narrow snout and the large, laterally placed eyes make it quite conspicuous and it is common throughout its range. There is a crest of sharp denticles under the tail, giving it the name Sawtail. It is found at depths of between 130 and 800 m.

Size Up to 60 cm.
Distribution Southern Australia.
Food Bottom-living fish, shellfish and squid.
Breeding Unknown.
Danger to humans Not known to be dangerous.

Australian Sawtail Catshark

BLACKMOUTH DOGFISH *Galeus melastomus*

This dogfish or catshark is primarily used for human consumption, and is a common catch in bottom trawls at depths of between 50 and 1000 m. The body is stout and has well-defined saddle markings and blotches. The dorsal fins and tail are tipped with white, but the mouth is dark, giving this species its name.

Blackmouth Dogfish

Size Up to 90 cm.
Distribution NE Atlantic and Mediterranean.
Food Mostly bottom-living shellfish, squid and some fish.
Breeding Live-bearer, up to 13 eggs in the female at a time.
Danger to humans Not known to be dangerous.

African Sawtail Catshark *Galeus polli*

This little catshark is recognised by the dark saddle markings, long, pointed snout and relatively squat body. The large eyes are an adaptation to its deep-water (to depths of 720 m), bottom-living lifestyle. Despite its name, it does not have a rough tail.

Size Up to 42 cm.
Distribution West coast of Africa.
Food Probably bottom-living invertebrates.
Breeding No recorded information.
Danger to humans Not known to be dangerous.

African Sawtail Catshark

Speckled Catshark *Halaelurus boesemani*

This small catshark is yellowish-brown with darker saddles. The snout is flattened and pointed and the 2 dorsal fins are of equal size. The body is marked with saddles and spots. A wide-ranging, bottom-living shark, found to depths of 250 m.

Speckled Catshark

↑

Size Up to 48 cm.
Distribution Arabian Gulf, Philippines, Indonesia and tropical W Africa.
Food Probably bottom-living invertebrates.
Breeding Not known.

Danger to humans Not known to be dangerous.

LINED CATSHARK *Halaelurus lineatus*

This small shark is pale brown with 26 bold vertical stripes. It has a short, pointed snout with an up-turned knob on it. A common species in warm temperate water where it lives over the sea floor to depths of 290 m.

Size Up to 56 cm.
Distribution South-eastern Africa.
Food Mostly bottom-living shellfish, and fish.
Breeding Pregnant females are common, and eggs have hatched in an aquarium after 36 days, but no eggs have been found in the wild.
Danger to humans Not known to be dangerous.

Lined Catshark

TIGER CATSHARK *Halaelurus natalensis*

A striking catshark, yellow-brown above and cream below with 10 pairs of broad, dark brown bars. This pattern is unique to this species. The pointed snout is upturned at the tip. Normally found on or near the sea floor over the S African continental shelf.

Tiger Catshark

Size Up to 47 cm.
Distribution Western Indian Ocean and S Africa.
Food Small bony fish, crabs, squid and other sharks.
Breeding Lays eggs.
Danger to humans Not known to be dangerous.

Puff Adder Shyshark *Haploblepharus edwardsii*

A golden-brown shark patterned with saddle markings and dark and light splotches. The numerous white spots and the dorsal fin positioned over or behind the pelvic fins are characteristic of this species. It occurs on sand and rock and is common between the shore and depths of 130 m.

Size Up to 60 cm.
Distribution S Africa.
Food Mostly bottom-living bony fish, shellfish, squid and worms.
Breeding Lays 2 egg cases at once; each has hair filaments that anchor it to the rocks.
Danger to humans Not known to be dangerous.

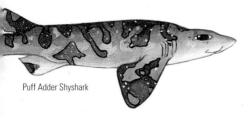

Puff Adder Shyshark

AFRICAN SPOTTED CATSHARK *Holohalaelurus punctatus*

The females of this species outnumber males and catches are all of one sex, which suggests that the sexes live in separate groups and only congregate to breed. The broad, flattened head, and closely spaced, dark brown spots on the body are characteristic of this species, which is commonly found on the continental slope.

African Spotted Catshark

Size Up to 34 cm.
Distribution South-eastern coasts of Africa.
Food Bottom-living bony fish, shellfish, octopus and squid.
Breeding
Live-bearer.
Danger to
humans Not
known to be
dangerous.

STRIPED CATSHARK *Poroderma africanum*

This catshark often rests in caves during the day but is active at night. The stripes down the length of the body and barbels over the nostrils are characteristic of this common shark. It is a robust species that is readily kept in captivity, where it is known to breed. This species is regularly caught by bottom trawlers and inshore anglers.

Size Up to 1 m.
Distribution Temperate southern Africa, Madagascar and possibly Mauritius.
Food Bottom-living shellfish and bony fish.
Breeding Lays eggs, which hatch after 9.5 months.
Danger to humans Not known to be dangerous.

Striped Catshark

Barbeled Catshark *Poroderma marleyi*

A short, squat-bodied catshark with a pale grey body and conspicuous dark spots. The long barbels under the snout give this shark its name. Little is known about this bottom-living species, as it has only been described from 5 specimens.

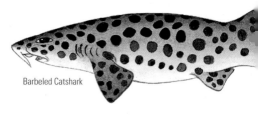

Barbeled Catshark

↑
Size Up to 65 cm.
Distribution Temperate south-eastern Africa.
Food Unknown.
Breeding Unknown.
Danger to humans Not known to be dangerous.

LEOPARD CATSHARK *Poroderma pantherinum*

A beautiful catshark with variable leopard-like markings covering the body. This species is a regular feature of shark tanks in large aquaria. In the wild it is found between the shore and depths of 250 m. It lives in caves and crevices during the day, but is active at night.

Size Up to 84 cm.
Distribution Temperate southern Africa and Madagascar.
Food Bottom-living bony fish, octopus and squid.
Breeding Lays eggs.
Danger to humans Not known to be dangerous.

Leopard Catshark

NARROWMOUTHED CATSHARK *Schroederichthys bivius*

The male Narrowmouthed Catshark has larger teeth than the female, used for grasping during courtship and mating. The colour is variable but is mostly grey-brown with saddle markings and a few widely scattered dark and light spots. This common inshore shark is found to depths of about 80 m.

Narrowmouthed Catshark

↑

Size Up to 70 cm.
Distribution Temperate S America.
Food Unknown.
Breeding Lays eggs, probably producing 1 at a time.
Danger to humans Not known to be dangerous.

LESSER SPOTTED DOGFISH *Scyliorhinus canicula*

An important commercial fishery exists off the British Isles for this abundant species, where it is caught for human consumption and sold as 'rock salmon'. It has a variable colour pattern, combining dark saddles, dark bars and combinations of light and dark spots. It prefers shallow water over sand and mud to depths of about 400 m and occasionally congregates near reefs where groups may be found resting. This species is most active at night.

Size Up to 1 m.

Distribution NE Atlantic and Mediterranean.

Food Mostly bottom-living shellfish and sea snails, occasionally bristleworms and fish.

Breeding Lays amber-coloured eggs with long tendrils. They hatch after 7–9 months.

Danger to humans Its rough skin can abrade when this fish is handled; otherwise it is too small to be dangerous.

Lesser Spotted Dogfish

YELLOW SPOTTED CATSHARK *Scyliorhinus capensis*

This shark has bright yellow spots and grey saddle markings, with the saddles more conspicuous in adults. The slender body is covered in large, erect denticles that make the skin rough to touch. This common shark is known to occupy rocky reef areas.

Yellow Spotted Catshark

Size Up to 1.2 m.
Distribution Eastern S Africa.
Food Bottom-living fish, shellfish and squid.
Breeding Lays characteristic 'mermaid purses', which take 7–9 months to hatch.
Danger to humans Not known to be dangerous.

CHAIN CATSHARK *Scyliorhinus retifer*

A common, deep-water catshark with striking bold black markings on the body. This species lives on rough, rocky areas to depths of 550 m, and is most abundant in rocky areas where trawling is virtually impossible.

Size Up to 50 cm.
Distribution Western N Atlantic and Caribbean.
Food Probably bottom-living invertebrates. Stomachs may contain small pebbles, which may act as ballast.
Breeding Lays eggs, and is believed to use specific areas to rear the young.
Danger to humans Not known to be dangerous.

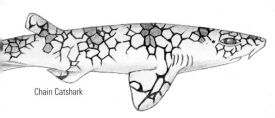

Chain Catshark

NURSEHOUND *Scyliorhinus stellaris*

A large, stocky dogfish with dark brown stippled markings and faint saddles on a pale body. It lives inshore, occupying reefs, where individuals may be found literally stacked one on top of another. This species can be found at depths from 1 m to at least 125 m, preferring areas covered in seaweed.

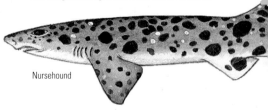

Nursehound

Size Up to 1.6 m.
Distribution NE Atlantic and Mediterranean.
Food Mostly shellfish, but also bottom-living fish.
Breeding Lays eggs with thick walls that take 9 months to hatch.
Danger to humans Not known to be dangerous.

CLOUDY CATSHARK *Scyliorhinus torazame*

A small, slender catshark with faint, dusky-brown saddle markings that are not outlined by spots or lines, and with irregular pale and dark spots. It is commonly found inshore to depths of 100 m.

Size Up to 50 cm.
Distribution Western N Pacific.
Food Probably bottom-living invertebrates.
Breeding Lays eggs that are deposited in specific areas used to rear the young (nurseries).
Danger to humans Not known to be dangerous.

Cloudy Catshark

Pygmy Ribbontail Catshark *Eridacnis radcliffei*

Pygmy Ribbontail Catshark

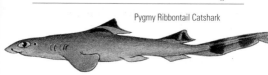

This is one of the smallest sharks. The body is brown with dark bands on the tail. The mouth is triangular and it has relatively large eyes enabling it to see prey in the low light levels at depths of up to 750 m.

Size Up to 25 cm.
Distribution Widespread, scattered in tropical Indo-Pacific.
Food Bony fish, particularly lantern fish, shellfish and squid.
Breeding Live-bearer with 1 or 2 young, born 10 cm long.
Danger to humans Too small to be dangerous.

FALSE CATSHARK *Pseudotriakis microdon*

This large, bulky, bottom-living shark has a soft body and is mostly inactive. The eyes are cat-like and the spiracles behind the eyes are large. It is found at depths of up to 1500 m, and occasionally in shallow water.

Size Up to 3 m.
Distribution Scattered worldwide in tropical and temperate waters.
Food Little known, but possibly bottom-living fish and invertebrates.
Breeding Live-bearer, with litters of 2–4 pups. Developing young are believed to eat others before they are born (uterine cannibalism) but this has not been proven in this species.
Danger to humans Not known to be dangerous.

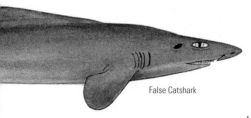

False Catshark

Barbeled Houndshark *Leptocharias smithii*

This slender, light grey or grey-brown shark is mostly found in inshore water to depths of 75 m. It shows a preference for muddy areas so it is often most abundant around river mouths.

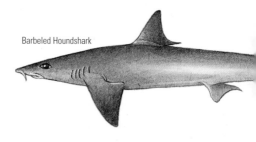

Barbeled Houndshark

↑
Size Up to 82 cm.
Distribution Eastern tropical Atlantic.
Food Bottom-living fish and shellfish.
Breeding Live-bearer, with litters of up to 7 young. Males have larger teeth, possibly used to bite females during mating.
Danger to humans Not known to be dangerous.

WHISKERY SHARK *Furgaleus macki*

A stocky, hump-backed shark with flaps over the nostrils that look like barbels. The body is grey above and pale below. The young and some adults have dark saddles. The snout is short, rounded or wedge-shaped. It is an active predator, living in or near the sea floor at moderate depths.

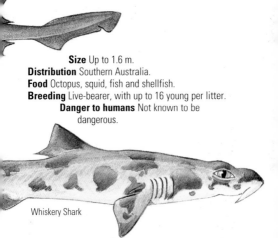

Size Up to 1.6 m.
Distribution Southern Australia.
Food Octopus, squid, fish and shellfish.
Breeding Live-bearer, with up to 16 young per litter.
Danger to humans Not known to be dangerous.

Whiskery Shark

119

TOPE *Galeorhinus galeus*

A large, grey, long-nosed shark with a conspicuous first dorsal fin. It is often found in shallow bays or marine canyons to depths of 500 m. This shark is a strong swimmer and can travel over 50 km a day.

Tope

↑
Size Up to 2 m.
Distribution Worldwide in tropical and temperate seas.
Food Schooling bony fish, bottom-living fish, octopus and squid.
Breeding Live-bearer, with up to 50 young per litter.
Danger to humans The sharp teeth should be respected, although there are no reported attacks.

JAPANESE TOPE _Hemitriakis japanica_

A grey, slender shark with a flattened, pointed snout and broadly arched mouth. The eyes are narrow and slit-like. It is common in temperate and tropical seas to depths of 100 m.

Size Up to 1.2 m.
Distribution Japan and W Pacific.
Food Fish, octopus, squid and shellfish.
Breeding Live-bearer, with up to 22 young per litter.
Danger to humans Not known to be dangerous.

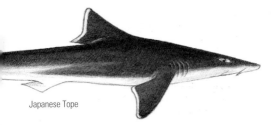

Japanese Tope

BIGEYE HOUNDSHARK *Iago omanensis*

A long-snouted houndshark with large dorsal and pectoral fins. The body is brown or grey above, pale below and has no obvious markings. It is found in deep, tropical water on the continental slope, possibly to depths of 2200 m in the Red Sea.

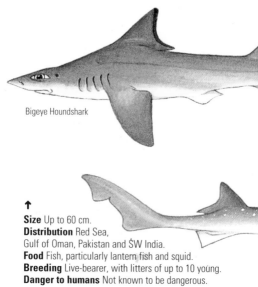

Bigeye Houndshark

↑

Size Up to 60 cm.
Distribution Red Sea,
Gulf of Oman, Pakistan and SW India.
Food Fish, particularly lantern fish and squid.
Breeding Live-bearer, with litters of up to 10 young.
Danger to humans Not known to be dangerous.

GUMMY SHARK *Mustelus antarcticus*

This shark is characterised by the pointed snout, large dorsal and pectoral fins and white spots on the grey-brown body. It is found near the sea floor to depths of 200 m. This shark is abundant in Australian waters where it is an important commercial species.

Size Up to 1.5 m.
Distribution Temperate Australia.
Food Mainly bottom-living invertebrates and small fish.
Breeding Live-bearer, with up to 16 young per litter.
Danger to humans Not known to be dangerous.

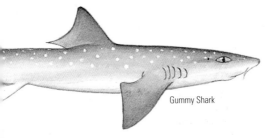

Gummy Shark

STARRY SMOOTHHOUND *Mustelus asterias*

The white spots on grey-brown skin gives this slender smoothhound its name. It has a preference for inshore waters over gravel to depths of 100 m. This fish and its close relative the Smoothhound (p. 132) are popular with anglers.

Starry Smoothhound

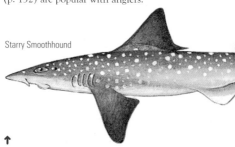

↑

Size Up to 1.4 m.
Distribution NE Atlantic and Mediterranean.
Food Mainly bottom-living shellfish.
Breeding Gestation can take up to 12 months.
Live-bearer, with up
to 15 pups per litter.
Danger to humans
Not known to be dangerous.

GREY SMOOTHHOUND *Mustelus californicus*

A uniformly grey, slender smoothhound with a pointed snout. It is commonly found offshore, migrating inshore in summer months. It is a schooling species, living over the sea floor.

Size Up to 1.25 m.
Distribution Warm temperate E Pacific, off California.
Food Mostly crabs and occasionally small fish.
Breeding Live-bearer, with up to 5 pups per litter.
Danger to humans Not known to be dangerous.

Grey Smoothhound

125

Dusky Smoothhound *Mustelus canis*

An abundant, active and voracious predator, this shark has a slender, uniform grey body that fades to a pale underside. It schools at depths to 600 m, and some occupy estuaries, but most are associated with rocky areas.

Dusky Smoothhound

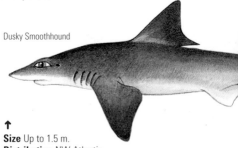

↑
Size Up to 1.5 m.
Distribution NW Atlantic, Caribbean and S America.
Food Mainly crabs and lobsters, but may eat small inshore fish and sea snails.
Breeding Mating occurs in mid-summer. Gestation is about 10 months. Live-bearer, with up to 20 pups in a litter.
Danger to humans Not known to be dangerous.

SPOTLESS SMOOTHHOUND *Mustelus griseus*

A smooth, uniformly grey shark with a short head and pointed snout. It lives over the sea floor to 75 m, not showing a preference for any particular habitat.

Size Up to 1 m.
Distribution Temperate W Pacific.
Food Mostly shellfish.
Breeding Gestation takes 9–10 months. Live-bearer, with up to 15 young per litter.
Danger to humans Not known to be dangerous.

Spotless Smoothhound

Brown Smoothhound *Mustelus henlei*

A bronze smoothhound with a pale underside. It is a voracious and agile predator that is abundant inshore and is associated with muddy bays, to depths of 200 m. It is a schooling species that undergoes local, seasonal migrations.

Brown Smoothhound

Size Up to 1 m.
Distribution Temperate eastern Pacific.
Food Bottom-living crabs and shrimps and occasionally small fish.
Breeding Live-bearer, with 5 young per litter.
Danger to humans Not known to be dangerous.

Spotted Estuary Smoothhound *Mustelus lenticulatus*

This white-spotted smoothhound is characterised by the large pectoral fins. It is a common, bottom-living species found to depths of 250 m. Occurring in schools, this species undergoes seasonal migrations, retreating to deeper water in winter. Of considerable commercial importance, this shark is caught mainly for human consumption, and is also popular with sports anglers.

Size Up to 1.4 m.
Distribution New Zealand.
Food Mainly bottom-living shellfish.
Breeding Gestation up to 11 months. Over 20 young produced per litter, depending on size of female.
Danger to humans Not known to be dangerous.

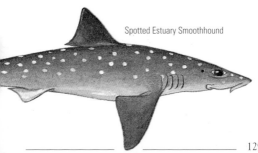

Spotted Estuary Smoothhound

STARSPOTTED SMOOTHHOUND *Mustelus manazo*

Many white spots cover the slender body of this grey-brown shark. An abundant inshore species, this fish is found over sand and mud. An important catch in Japan, China and Taiwan, where it is used for human consumption.

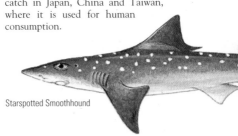

Starspotted Smoothhound

↑
Size Up to 1.2 m.
Distribution Western Pacific and Indian Ocean.
Food Bottom-living crabs, shrimps and small fish.
Breeding Live-bearer, with about 5 young per litter, but may have as many as 20.
Danger to humans Not known to be dangerous.

ARABIAN SMOOTHHOUND *Mustelus mosis*

This uniformly grey smoothhound has no spots but it has a short, pointed snout and prominent dorsal fin. A common inshore species that lives close to the sea floor on reefs and in bays. An important food species off India and Pakistan.

Size Up to 1.5 m.
Distribution Western and northern Indian Ocean and Red Sea.
Food Bottom-living crabs, sea snails and small fish.
Breeding Live-bearer, with up to 10 young per litter.
Danger to humans Not known to be dangerous.

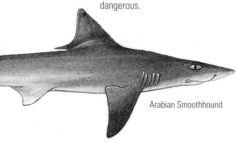

Arabian Smoothhound

131

SMOOTHHOUND *Mustelus mustelus*

A slender, grey smoothhound with a broad, pointed snout and relatively large eyes. Abundant at depths to 350 m and found mainly over sand and mud, it is occasionally caught in mid-water. A voracious and active predator, it often occurs in large schools and undergoes seasonal migrations. An important commercial species, trawled and netted for human consumption and fishmeal.

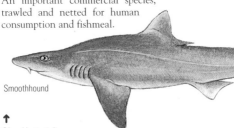

Smoothhound

↑
Size Up to 1.6 m.
Distribution Eastern Atlantic, from the British Isles to southern Africa.
Food Bottom-living crabs and sea snails, occasionally octopus, squid and small fish.
Breeding Live-bearer, with up to 15 pups per litter.
Danger to humans Not known to be dangerous.

WHITESPOTTED SMOOTHHOUND *Mustelus palumbes*

This shark is considered excellent meat, dried as 'biltong'. Comparatively large for a smoothhound, it is recognised by the broad, pointed snout, large triangular pectoral fins and uniform grey or grey-brown body. A common inshore species living at depths to 350 m over sand and gravel, it is commercially important.

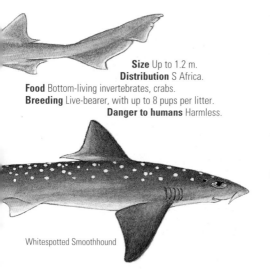

Size Up to 1.2 m.
Distribution S Africa.
Food Bottom-living invertebrates, crabs.
Breeding Live-bearer, with up to 8 pups per litter.
Danger to humans Harmless.

Whitespotted Smoothhound

SHARPTOOTH HOUNDSHARK *Triakis megalopterus*

A large shark with characteristic small black spots on a grey-brown body, and large dorsal and pectoral fins. Commonly found inshore, often associated with sandy shores and rocks. It sometimes aggregates in schools in summer months. Dried as 'biltong' for human consumption.

Sharptooth Houndshark

↑
Size Up to 1.75 m.
Distribution S Africa.
Food Bottom-living crabs, fish and small sharks.
Breeding Live-bearer, with up to 12 pups per litter.
Danger to humans Not known to be dangerous, but care is needed when handling.

LEOPARD SHARK *Triakis semifasciata*

Not to be confused with the Leopard Catshark (p.109), this shark also has broad saddle markings down the back. It is a common inshore species found over muddy and sandy areas at depths to 100 m. Occasionally it occurs in large schools. Does well in captivity.

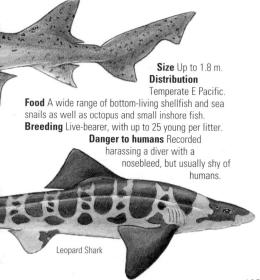

Size Up to 1.8 m.
Distribution Temperate E Pacific.
Food A wide range of bottom-living shellfish and sea snails as well as octopus and small inshore fish.
Breeding Live-bearer, with up to 25 young per litter.
Danger to humans Recorded harassing a diver with a nosebleed, but usually shy of humans.

Leopard Shark

HOOKTOOTH SHARK *Chaenogaleus macrostoma*

A slender greyish shark with pointed pectoral fins, a pointed snout and conspicuous teeth in a crescent-shaped mouth. Like most common inshore sharks living over shelf areas, it is caught in local fisheries, on lines and in gill nets.

Hooktooth Shark

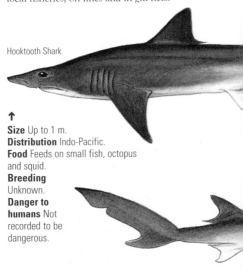

↑
Size Up to 1 m.
Distribution Indo-Pacific.
Food Feeds on small fish, octopus and squid.
Breeding Unknown.
Danger to humans Not recorded to be dangerous.

SICKLEFIN WEASELSHARK *Hemigaleus microstoma*

The crescent-shaped fins and elongated, pale grey body of this shark give it its name. Relatively common in inshore waters throughout its range, it is an active hunter of octopus and squid.

Size Up to 90 cm.
Distribution W Indo-Pacific and northern Australia.
Food Octopus and squid.
Breeding Live-bearer, with up to 19 pups per litter.
Danger to humans Not known to be dangerous.

Sicklefin Weaselshark

137

SNAGGLETOOTH SHARK *Hemipristis elongatus*

Rightly called the snaggletooth, this large shark has very conspicuous teeth in the crescent-shaped mouth. The body is pale grey or bronze. It is an inshore mid-water species.

Snaggletooth Shark

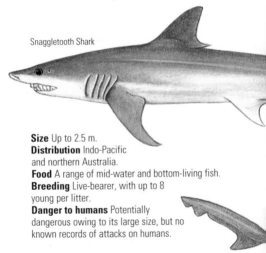

Size Up to 2.5 m.
Distribution Indo-Pacific and northern Australia.
Food A range of mid-water and bottom-living fish.
Breeding Live-bearer, with up to 8 young per litter.
Danger to humans Potentially dangerous owing to its large size, but no known records of attacks on humans.

ATLANTIC WEASELSHARK *Paragaleus pectoralis*

Called a weaselshark because of the elongated snout and body and slender pectoral fins. The body is pale grey or bronze with yellow bands running lengthways. A common, active, inshore species occurring in schools.

Size Up to 1.4 m.
Distribution On the eastern tropical Atlantic.
Food Squid and octopus, occasionally small bony fish.
Breeding Live-bearer, with up to 4 pups per litter.
Danger to humans Not known to be dangerous.

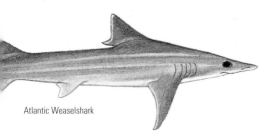

Atlantic Weaselshark

BLACKNOSE SHARK *Carcharhinus acronotus*

This is a fast, active, mid-water shark with an elongated blunt snout marked with a dark tip, hence its name. The teeth are fine and jagged, designed for catching its prey of fish or octopus over coral and sand. It displays a characteristic hunched-back threat display when being aggressive to other sharks or divers.

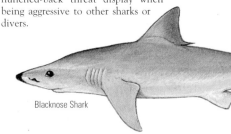

Blacknose Shark

↑
Size Up to 2 m.
Distribution Western tropical and warm temperate Atlantic.
Food Mainly bottom-living fish and octopus.
Breeding Live-bearer, with litters of up to 4 young that take 2 years to mature.
Danger to humans Has threatened divers, and large size commands respect.

SILVERTIP SHARK *Carcharhinus albimarginatus*

A large, grey shark with conspicuous white edges to
the fins. Common in coastal mid-water where it
occurs to depths of 800 m and is often associated
with coral reefs. The young prefer shallow water
and they are known to be aggressive to their own
species.

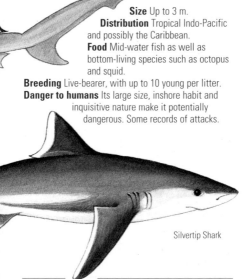

Size Up to 3 m.
Distribution Tropical Indo-Pacific
and possibly the Caribbean.
Food Mid-water fish as well as
bottom-living species such as octopus
and squid.
Breeding Live-bearer, with up to 10 young per litter.
Danger to humans Its large size, inshore habit and
inquisitive nature make it potentially
dangerous. Some records of attacks.

Silvertip Shark

BIGNOSE SHARK *Carcharhinus altimus*

A large, grey-brown species with a blunt snout ('big nose'). The pectoral fins are long, as is the tail, which has dark marks on the tip. Adults are normally found offshore, living at depths to 450 m, although young are found in shallower water.

Bignose Shark

Size Up to 3 m.
Distribution Widely distributed in tropical and warm temperate seas.
Food Mainly bottom-living fish and sharks.
Breeding Live-bearer, with up to 15 pups per litter.
Danger to humans Potentially dangerous, but unlikely to be encountered by humans.

GRACEFUL SHARK *Carcharhinus amblyrhynchoides*

A deep-bodied, grey shark with a short pointed snout, large eyes and dark tips to fins and tail. This species is commonly found in mangroves and reefs. It may be solitary or occur in groups and is known to move further inshore at night.

Size Up to 1.7 m.
Distribution Northern Indian Ocean, Micronesia and northern Australia.
Food Mostly inshore bony fish, including many bottom-living species; also shellfish, octopus and squid.
Breeding Live-bearer. Litter size unknown.
Danger to humans Not usually aggressive.

Graceful Shark

GREY REEF SHARK *Carcharhinus amblyrhynchos*

The Grey Reef Shark is inquisitive, gregarious and exhibits aggressive hunched-back behaviour when agitated. It is most commonly found over reefs in lagoons and areas with strong currents, although it may go as deep as 100 m.

Grey Reef Shark

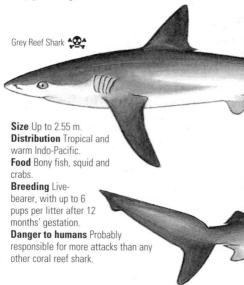

Size Up to 2.55 m.
Distribution Tropical and warm Indo-Pacific.
Food Bony fish, squid and crabs.
Breeding Live-bearer, with up to 6 pups per litter after 12 months' gestation.
Danger to humans Probably responsible for more attacks than any other coral reef shark.

COPPER SHARK *Carcharhinus brachyurus*

This large, bronze-coloured shark has a long, rounded snout, long pectoral fins and sharp, jagged teeth. It is commonly found in inshore waters to depths of 100 m and may undergo extensive migrations.

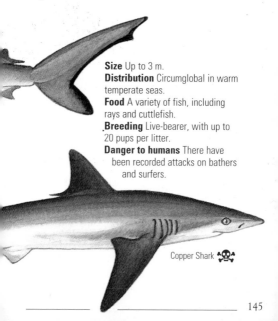

Size Up to 3 m.
Distribution Circumglobal in warm temperate seas.
Food A variety of fish, including rays and cuttlefish.
Breeding Live-bearer, with up to 20 pups per litter.
Danger to humans There have been recorded attacks on bathers and surfers.

Copper Shark

145

SPINNER SHARK *Carcharhinus brevipinna*

A large, grey shark, characterised by black tips to the fins, which feeds by spinning through schools of fish, snapping in all directions and occasionally leaping from the water. It makes annual migrations and is found to depths of 75 m, but is more commonly found in schools in shallow water.

Spinner Shark

↑

Size Up to 2.8 m.
Distribution
Circumglobal in tropical
and warm temperate seas.
Food Wide range of mid-water
and bottom-living fish and squid.
Breeding Live-bearer, with up to 15 pups
per litter.
Danger to humans At least 1 record of
attacking a bather, and known to be
troublesome to spear fishermen.

SILKY SHARK *Carcharhinus falciformis*

A streamlined, grey shark with a long, rounded snout and fine, triangular, jagged teeth. This is an abundant species inshore and offshore at depths to 500 m and is known to pursue tuna.

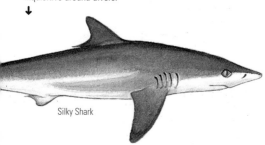

Size Up to 3.3 m.
Distribution Circumglobal in tropical and warm temperate seas.
Food Mid-water and bottom-living fish, squid and crabs.
Breeding Live-bearer, with up to 14 young per litter.
Danger to humans Potentially dangerous and inquisitive around divers.

↓

Silky Shark

GALAPAGOS SHARK *Carcharhinus galapagensis*

A large, heavy-bodied, grey shark that is known to occupy inshore and offshore waters to depths of 200 m, but is mostly found in groups around offshore islands. This species displays the aggressive hunched-back posture preceding an attack.

Galapagos Shark

Size Up to 3.7 m.
Distribution Patchy distribution, circumglobal, mostly associated with oceanic islands.
Food Bottom-living fish and squid, but will take a variety of baits.
Breeding Live-bearer, with up to 16 young per litter.
Danger to humans Attacks recorded on divers and known to show 'feeding frenzies'. Young may charge divers without provocation.

PONDICHERRY SHARK *Carcharhinus hemiodon*

A grey shark that has a wide-ranging distribution, and is thought to be common. Reports of this species have come from river deltas and estuaries and they are fished for in the Arabian Sea and off the coasts of India.

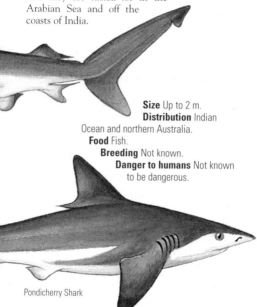

Size Up to 2 m.
Distribution Indian Ocean and northern Australia.
Food Fish.
Breeding Not known.
Danger to humans Not known to be dangerous.

Pondicherry Shark

149

BULL SHARK *Carcharhinus leucas*

Its abundance, wide geographical distribution and the size and variety of prey items make this species the most dangerous to humans. The large, heavy body and broad, triangular teeth set in massive jaws make it a formidable predator. It is found in coastal waters to depths of 150 m, is often associated with muddy estuaries and river mouths, and may even occur in freshwater.

↑

Size Up to 3.4 m.
Distribution Circumglobal in tropical and warm temperate seas.

Bull Shark

Food Bony fish, sharks and rays. Turtles, sea birds, dolphins, antelope, cattle, people, tree sloths, dogs and rats have also been recorded in Bull Shark stomachs.
Breeding Live-bearer, with up to 13 young per litter.
Danger to humans The most dangerous shark. It takes large prey and occurs near human habitation.

BLACKTIP SHARK *Carcharhinus limbatus*

This large, stout-bodied shark has a pale brown, bronze body and characteristic dark markings on the tips of the fins. A highly active and gregarious inshore species, it is found associated with muddy bays, estuaries and mangrove areas, but is rarely seen below 30 m.

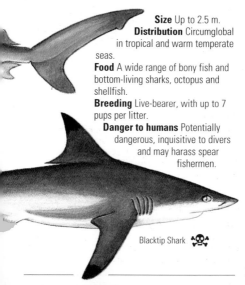

Size Up to 2.5 m.
Distribution Circumglobal in tropical and warm temperate seas.
Food A wide range of bony fish and bottom-living sharks, octopus and shellfish.
Breeding Live-bearer, with up to 7 pups per litter.
Danger to humans Potentially dangerous, inquisitive to divers and may harass spear fishermen.

Blacktip Shark

OCEANIC WHITETIP SHARK *Carcharhinus longimanus*

A large, grey-bronze, blunt-nosed shark with very large pectoral, dorsal and tail fins, which have white edges. A widespread oceanic species that is only occasionally found in coastal waters. It cruises near the surface, is capable of good acceleration and is known to be aggressive to other sharks when competing for food.

Oceanic Whitetip Shark

↑
Size Up to 4 m.
Distribution Circumglobal in tropical seas.
Food Oceanic fish, sea birds, turtles and dolphins.
Breeding Live-bearer, with up to 15 pups per litter.
Danger to humans A dangerous shark, but its slow approach enables bathers to retreat to safety. Stubborn and aggressive, this shark should be treated with extreme care. Believed responsible for large numbers of deaths when ships sink at sea.

HARDNOSE SHARK *Carcharhinus macloti*

A slender, grey or grey-brown shark with a long, pointed nose and relatively large eyes. It is found in inshore waters and in some areas 95% of catches are males. Similar catches of females have not been reported, but it is believed that they also occur in groups.

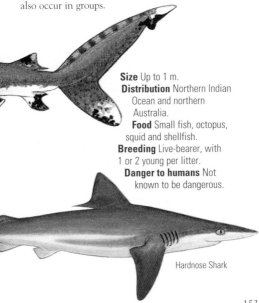

Size Up to 1 m.
Distribution Northern Indian Ocean and northern Australia.
Food Small fish, octopus, squid and shellfish.
Breeding Live-bearer, with 1 or 2 young per litter.
Danger to humans Not known to be dangerous.

Hardnose Shark

153

BLACKTIP REEF SHARK *Carcharhinus melanopterus*

The characteristic black tips to the fins and tail mean this shark is easy to identify. It is very abundant over reefs, in shallow lagoons, mangrove areas and tidal channels where it is found in large schools. It undergoes tidal migrations often within a limited territorial range of a few square kilometres.

Blacktip Reef Shark

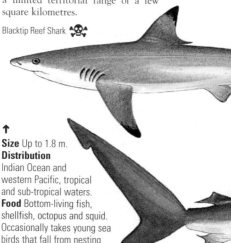

↑
Size Up to 1.8 m.
Distribution Indian Ocean and western Pacific, tropical and sub-tropical waters.
Food Bottom-living fish, shellfish, octopus and squid. Occasionally takes young sea birds that fall from nesting sites.
Breeding Live-bearer, with up to 4 young per litter.
Danger to humans Known to attack humans wading in very shallow murky waters.

Dusky Shark *Carcharhinus obscurus*

This big, grey shark has large, crescent-shaped pectoral fins. It commonly frequents coasts and is often seen following ships. A strongly migratory fish, it moves north in summer and south in winter. Immature sharks leave breeding areas in single sex groups, often migrating in different directions.

Size Up to 4 m.
Distribution Circumglobal in tropical and warm temperate seas.
Food A wide range of mid-water and bottom-living sharks and rays. Also takes crabs, lobsters, squid and octopus. A general scavenger.
Breeding Live-bearer, with up to 14 pups per litter.
Danger to humans Potentially dangerous and has been involved in several persistent attacks on swimmers.

Dusky Shark

155

Caribbean Reef Shark *Carcharhinus perezi*

This large, grey shark has a short, blunt snout and no distinct markings. It is one of the commonest reef sharks seen over sand and near steep reefs in the Caribbean. It is known to aggregate in numbers in caves where it rests.

Caribbean Reef Shark

↑

Size Up to 3 m.
Distribution Caribbean.
Food A wide range of fish.
Breeding Live-bearer, with up to 6 young per litter.
Danger to humans Has been responsible for a number of attacks, although not usually aggressive.

SANDBAR SHARK *Carcharhinus plumbeus*

This greyish shark has an extremely tall first dorsal fin. It is commonly associated with bays and harbours, but may be found further out to sea, to depths of 280 m. An annual migration in the western N Atlantic takes this species north in summer and south in winter. Usually the sexes travel separately, the males leaving earlier and swimming at a greater depth.

Size Up to 3 m.
Distribution Circumglobal in tropical and warm temperate seas.
Food A wide range of fish and sharks.
Breeding Live-bearer, with up to 12 pups per litter.
Danger to humans Not usually aggressive.

Sandbar Shark

157

SMALLTAIL SHARK *Carcharhinus porosus*

A small, grey shark with a moderately long and pointed snout. The eyes are large and round. The teeth are broad and jagged, designed to catch and hold slippery fish. It is commonly associated with estuaries and inshore waters to depths of 36 m, but definitely prefers muddy areas.

Smalltail Shark

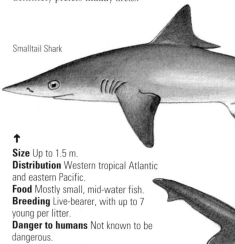

↑

Size Up to 1.5 m.
Distribution Western tropical Atlantic and eastern Pacific.
Food Mostly small, mid-water fish.
Breeding Live-bearer, with up to 7 young per litter.
Danger to humans Not known to be dangerous.

BLACKSPOT SHARK *Carcharhinus sealei*

This small, greyish shark is distinguished by a conspicuous black spot on the second dorsal fin and pale edges to the front of the other fins. There are no other markings. The eyes are large and oval. It is commonly found in coastal areas to depths of 40 m.

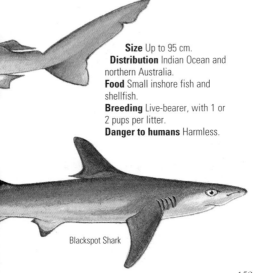

Size Up to 95 cm.
Distribution Indian Ocean and northern Australia.
Food Small inshore fish and shellfish.
Breeding Live-bearer, with 1 or 2 pups per litter.
Danger to humans Harmless.

Blackspot Shark

NIGHT SHARK *Carcharhinus signatus*

A large, grey shark with large eyes and a pointed snout. It is found in coastal waters between 50 and 600 m, preferring depths of between 50 and 100 m. This active species occurs in schools and undergoes vertical migrations throughout the day, following its prey.

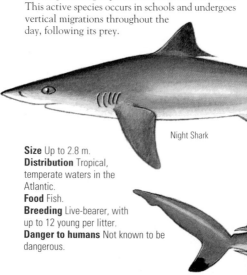

Night Shark

Size Up to 2.8 m.
Distribution Tropical, temperate waters in the Atlantic.
Food Fish.
Breeding Live-bearer, with up to 12 young per litter.
Danger to humans Not known to be dangerous.

SPOTTAIL SHARK *Carcharhinus sorrah*

A fast, deep-bodied shark with a medium-grey body and conspicuous black spots on the pectoral and second dorsal fins, and the tail. This is a common coastal species found around coral reefs to depths of 80 m.

Size Up to 1.6 m.
Distribution Indian Ocean and northern Australia.
Food Small reef fish, other sharks, shellfish, octopus and squid. Juveniles feed mostly over the sea bed.
Breeding Live-bearer, with up to 6 pups per litter.
Danger to humans Not known to be aggressive to humans.

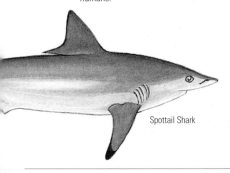

Spottail Shark

GROUND SHARKS

BLACKTAIL REEF SHARK *Carcharhinus wheeleri*

A stocky, grey shark with a long, rounded snout
and usually with round eyes. A common inshore
species, it is found from the shore to depths of 140
m. It is associated with coral reefs
and the young are known to
occupy shallow waters.

Blacktail Reef Shark

↑

Size Up to 1.9 m.
Distribution Red Sea and Indian Ocean.
Food Small fish, squid and octopus.
Breeding Live-bearer, with up to 4 young per
litter.
Danger to humans Potentially dangerous.

Tiger Shark

TIGER SHARK *Galeocerdo cuvier*

A large, blunt-snouted shark; the young have vertical stripes which fade in adults. The teeth are large, curved and heavily serrated. This wide-ranging species prefers inshore waters with low visibility, and is often associated with estuaries, harbours, atolls and lagoons. Although mainly nocturnal, it migrates inshore daily. It is often solitary, cruising slowly, but it is capable of high speeds.

Size Up to 6 m.

Distribution Circumglobal in warm temperate and tropical seas.

Food Unspecialised diet. Sometimes referred to as 'garbage can with fins' or 'sea hyena'. Takes many bony fish, including the toxic pufferfish, other sharks, turtles, sea snakes, sea birds, sea lions, dolphins, dogs and humans. Will eat a variety of human junk, including coal, wood, plastic and small barrels.

Breeding Lays eggs.

Danger to humans A very dangerous shark, with confirmed attacks on swimmers and boats (multiple attacks). Considered more dangerous than the Great White (p.84) in some areas. Reputation as a man-eater.

GANGES SHARK *Glyphis gangeticus*

A stocky, grey or brown shark with minute eyes and large dorsal and pectoral fins. A little-known species that lives in rivers and estuaries and also occurs in inshore waters. Its fearsome reputation of being a man-eater was based on a series of attacks incorrectly attributed to this species.

Ganges Shark

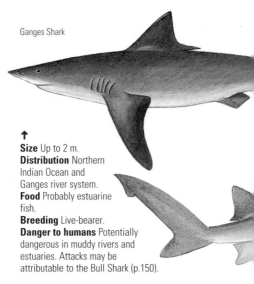

↑

Size Up to 2 m.
Distribution Northern Indian Ocean and Ganges river system.
Food Probably estuarine fish.
Breeding Live-bearer.
Danger to humans Potentially dangerous in muddy rivers and estuaries. Attacks may be attributable to the Bull Shark (p.150).

Lemon Shark *Negaprion brevirostris*

A large, yellow or brown shark with a broad, rounded snout and smooth, single-pointed teeth. It is commonly found inshore to depths of 100 m, often associated with mangroves, or found near docks and in the muddy waters of river mouths. It may be found singly or in groups and it undergoes seasonal migrations.

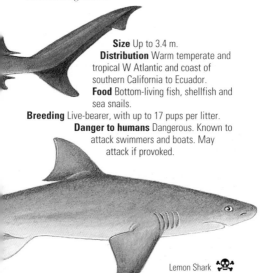

Size Up to 3.4 m.

Distribution Warm temperate and tropical W Atlantic and coast of southern California to Ecuador.

Food Bottom-living fish, shellfish and sea snails.

Breeding Live-bearer, with up to 17 pups per litter.

Danger to humans Dangerous. Known to attack swimmers and boats. May attack if provoked.

Lemon Shark

BLUE SHARK *Prionace glauca*

A long, sinuous, dark blue shark with a long, pointed snout, large eyes and long pectoral fins. This wide-ranging oceanic species undergoes extensive migrations north in summer and south in winter. It is either found swimming near the surface or to depths of 220 m.

Blue Shark

Size Up to 3.8 m.
Distribution Circumglobal in tropical and temperate seas.
Food Bony fish and squid, although known to scavenge.
Breeding Live-bearer, with up to 135 pups per litter.
Danger to humans A dangerous shark with confirmed attacks. Often circles divers.

MILK SHARK *Rhizoprionodon acutus*

This shark may be grey, brown or purple-brown. It is common inshore and found to depths of 200 m near sandy beaches and sometimes in the mouths of estuaries. It is often preyed on by other sharks whose decline has resulted in an increase in numbers of Milk Sharks. Given its name because in India its flesh was believed to stimulate lactation in women.

Size Up to 1.7 m.
Distribution Circumglobal off warm temperate and tropical coasts.
Food Mostly bottom-living fish, squid and shellfish.
Breeding Live-bearer, with 2–8 pups per litter.
Danger to humans Harmless to humans.

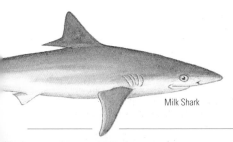

Milk Shark

CARIBBEAN SHARPNOSE SHARK *Rhizoprionodon porosus*

This small shark has a long, blunt snout and large eyes, and a brown or grey-brown body. It is a common, coastal species often found associated with sea grass beds in lagoons, coral reefs and occasionally estuaries. A shark that keeps well in large aquaria.

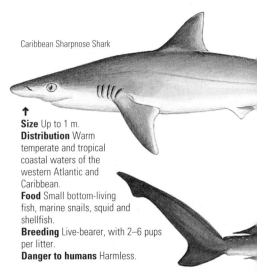

Caribbean Sharpnose Shark

↑

Size Up to 1 m.
Distribution Warm temperate and tropical coastal waters of the western Atlantic and Caribbean.
Food Small bottom-living fish, marine snails, squid and shellfish.
Breeding Live-bearer, with 2–6 pups per litter.
Danger to humans Harmless.

ATLANTIC SHARPNOSE SHARK *Rhizoprionodon terraenovae*

A medium-sized, grey or grey-brown shark with a
white underside. It prefers shallow water in the surf
of sandy beaches and is often associated with
estuaries where it penetrates into freshwater. This
species undergoes seasonal migrations, moving
offshore in winter and back inshore in spring. It is
found to depths of 280 m.

Size Up to 1.1 m.
Distribution Northern W
Atlantic.
Food Small mid-water and
bottom-living fish.
Breeding Live-bearer, with 4–6 pups per litter.
Danger to humans Harmless.

Atlantic Sharpnose Shark

Spadenose Shark *Scoliodon laticaudus*

The bronze-grey body and white underside have no obvious markings; however, the long, flat, spade-shaped snout makes this shark unmistakable. It is a common species found inshore, most often associated with rocky areas, estuaries and river mouths.

Spadenose Shark

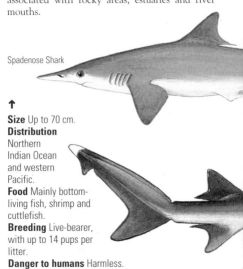

↑

Size Up to 70 cm.
Distribution Northern Indian Ocean and western Pacific.
Food Mainly bottom-living fish, shrimp and cuttlefish.
Breeding Live-bearer, with up to 14 pups per litter.
Danger to humans Harmless.

WHITETIP REEF SHARK *Triaenodon obesus*

A slender, grey shark with conspicuous white tips to the first dorsal and tail fins. This common inshore shark is found on or over coral reefs to depths of 300 m and is often associated with coral caves where it rests. This species does not travel far from its selected cave, although periodically it will move to a new one.

Size Up to 2 m.
Distribution Tropical Indo-Pacific.
Food Mainly feed on bottom-living reef fish, octopus and shellfish.
Breeding Live-bearer, with up to 5 pups per litter.
Danger to humans Rarely aggressive, but if harassed will bite.

Whitetip Reef Shark

WINGHEAD SHARK *Eusphyra blochii*

A tropical shark with a light grey or brown body and an unmistakable broad, wing-shaped head. The increased surface area of the winged head is believed to increase sensitivity to smell, taste and movement, and helps this hammerhead find its prey in the shallow waters and coastal inlets it inhabits.

Winghead Shark

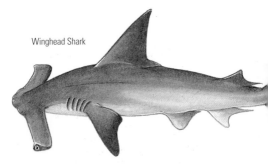

Size Up to 1.5 m.
Distribution Northern Indian Ocean and northern Australia.
Food Most likely small fish, octopus, squid and shellfish.
Breeding Live-bearer, commonly with 6 pups per litter.
Danger to humans Harmless.

SCALLOPED HAMMERHEAD *Sphyrna lewini*

A large, grey-brown hammerhead with a very high first dorsal fin and dark edges to the front of the tail fin. A migratory shark, this species is found in coastal waters where it enters bays and estuaries, often in large schools. It shows complex aggressive and courtship behaviour, with some evidence of social feeding.

Size Up to 4.2 m.

Distribution Circumglobal in tropical and warm temperate seas.

Food Mid-water and bottom-living fish, rays, shellfish, octopus and sometimes sea-snakes.

Breeding Live-bearer, commonly with 15–31 young per litter. Nursery areas are in muddy shallow waters.

Danger to humans Possibly dangerous, but may be confused with smooth hammerhead (p.176).

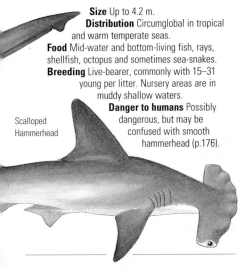

Scalloped Hammerhead

GREAT HAMMERHEAD *Sphyrna mokarran*

This is the largest hammerhead shark, recognised by its sheer size and a conspicuously high dorsal fin. The body is grey or brown. It is a nomadic shark found over the continental shelf, often associated with lagoons and coral atolls.

Great Hammerhead

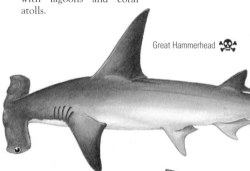

Size Up to 6.1 m.

Distribution Circumglobal in tropical and warm temperate seas.

Food Mostly bottom-living bony fish, sharks and rays, but occasionally shellfish. Often eats stingrays (p.236), and up to 50 stings were found in the mouth of one individual.

Breeding Live-bearer, with up to 42 young per litter.

Danger to humans Dangerous, reported to attack bathers and may make close passes at divers.

BONNETHEAD *Sphyrna tiburo*

A small, grey or grey-brown hammerhead with a narrow, shovel-shaped head without indentations. Abundant inshore, this shark is found over mud, sand and coral reefs, often near estuaries and bays. It may occur in large schools that undergo seasonal migrations, and exhibits complicated behaviour associated with courtship and maintenance of social position.

Size Up to 1.5 m.
Distribution Western Atlantic and eastern Pacific.
Food Mostly bottom-living shellfish; occasionally small fish.
Breeding Live-bearer, with up to 16 young per litter.
Danger to humans Not known to be dangerous.

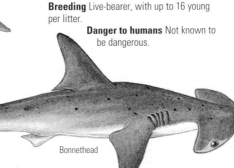

Bonnethead

Smooth Hammerhead *Sphyrna zygaena*

A large, dark grey, brown or sometimes olive hammerhead with a white underside. The most distinctive features are the broad blade-like head and high first dorsal fin. It is usually found over deep water, although at times it moves inshore. It sometimes occurs in enormous schools undergoing migrations to warmer water in the winter. This hammerhead is the most tolerant of temperate waters; however, it should not be assumed that all sightings made in temperate climes are of this species.

Smooth Hammerhead

Size Up to 4 m.
Distribution Circumglobal in tropical and warm
temperate seas.

Food Fish, including sharks and bottom-living
species as well as shellfish.
Breeding Live-bearer, with up to 37
young per litter.
Danger to humans Can be
aggressive, but few reported
attacks.

Angelsharks

This group (Squatinidae) is widely distributed in temperate and tropical waters. Angelsharks have flattened bodies, broad, lobed pectoral fins and spineless dorsal fins set back on the tail. The eyes and spiracles are on top of the head and the gill slits are situated on the sides. The mouth is highly expandable (protrusible) and sited at the very front of the head with conspicuous nasal barbels. Prey passing in front of the mouth is caught by a quick snap. Most angelsharks do not grow over 1.6 m, but some may reach over 2 m. They are bottom-living fish in mud and sand, but some are active swimmers at night. Some species are commercially fished and used for human consumption and other products. They are not dangerous to humans unless provoked; if hands or limbs are put near the head they may bite.

Sawback Angelshark *Squatina aculeata*

This angelshark is sandy-brown with symmetrically placed white spots. It has a characteristic flattened body with a row of small spines down the centre of the back. The head is broad and the nostrils have very small, branched tentacles. Rather little is known of this bottom-living fish, which occurs to depths of 200 m.

Size Up to 1.5 m.
Distribution Mediterranean and eastern Atlantic.
Food Bottom-living fish and shellfish.
Breeding Lays eggs.
Danger to humans Not known to be dangerous.

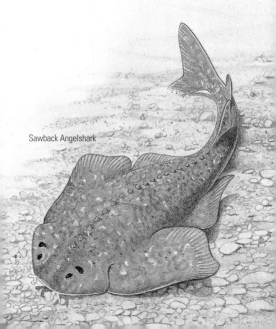

Sawback Angelshark

AFRICAN ANGELSHARK *Squatina africana*

An attractive angelshark, which has a reddish-brown, brown or grey back marbled with white spots and pale brown markings. The teeth are small with a single point. It is usually found on the sea floor, at depths of between 60 and 400 m.

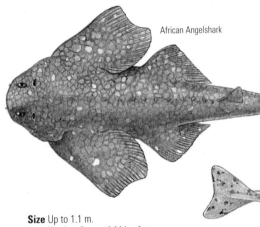

African Angelshark

Size Up to 1.1 m.
Distribution Coast of Africa from Lagos to Natal.
Food Not known.
Breeding Live-bearer, with 7–10 pups per litter, born at 30 cm long.
Danger to humans Not known to be dangerous.

PACIFIC ANGELSHARK *Squatina californica*

The broad pectoral fins and the rows of small tubercles (bumps) on the back are characteristic of this angelshark. The body is grey and has brown flecks of varying size. It is often found in sand or mud, near rocky reefs, to depths of 200 m, and is most active at night. This species is believed to be migratory, and forms schools.

Size Up to 1.5 m.
Distribution Eastern Pacific seaboard.
Food Bottom-living fish, sharks and shellfish. Prey is ambushed.
Breeding Live-bearer, with up to 13 young per litter.
Danger to humans May bite if harassed.

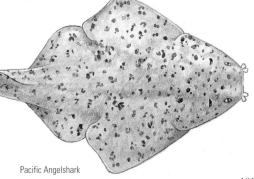

Pacific Angelshark

SMOOTHBACK ANGELSHARK *Squatina oculata*

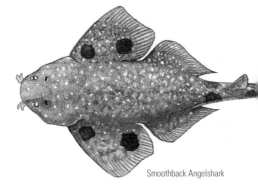

Smoothback Angelshark

This angelshark has a flattened body with distinctive spots. The underside is white and there are fringed tentacles on the nose. Little is known about this shark, except that it lives over sand and mud to depths of 30 m.

Size Up to 1.5 m.
Distribution Mediterranean and eastern Atlantic.
Food Bottom-living fish and shellfish.
Breeding Not known.
Danger to humans Not known to be dangerous, but may snap at a hand placed near the head.

ANGELSHARK *Squatina squatina*

This large grey or brown angelshark is an active swimmer but spends most of its time on the sea bed. It has a characteristic broad, flattened head and conspicuous rounded pectoral fins. It prefers sand and gravel sea floor, but it may be associated with rocky reefs to depths of 100 m.

Size Up to 2.5 m.
Distribution Mediterranean and eastern Atlantic.
Food Bottom-living fish, sea snails, squid and crabs.
Breeding Live-bearer, may have litters of up to 25.
Danger to humans Not considered dangerous, but may bite.

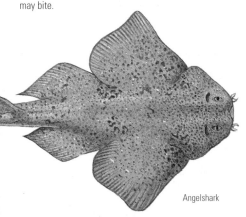

Angelshark

SAWFISH

Sawfish (Pristiformes) are large (some over 7 m) and circumglobal in distribution. The flattened, elongated bodies and blade-like snouts with paired teeth looking like a saw are adaptions to life on the sea floor, and are characteristic of this group. The gills are sited on the underside of the head and there are no barbels. They use the saw to stun and kill bottom-living prey. The teeth of the saw are continually growing, but if they are lost they are not replaced. In some areas sawfish are commercially important. Serious injury can result from close contact with sawfish.

NARROW SAWFISH *Anoxypristis cuspidata*

A slender sawfish that has a grey back and is pale underneath. There are 18–22 teeth on the long, narrow saw, but none at the base of the saw. The dorsal fins are pale and conspicuous and the tail fin has a large lower lobe. It has large eyes, and the nostrils are very narrow with small flaps. This species is of some local importance and is used for human consumption and liver oil.

Size Up to 3.5 m, but unconfirmed records to 6 m.
Distribution Indo-Pacific from the Red Sea to Japan and northern Australia.
Food Bottom-living schooling fish, crabs and shellfish.
Breeding Little information on this species.
Danger to humans Not known to be dangerous.

Narrow Sawfish

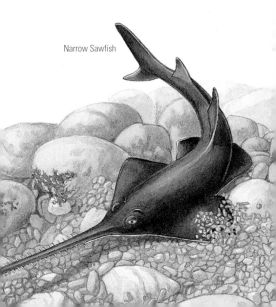

Sawfish *Pristis pectinata*

A very large sawfish with a uniformly blue-grey to olive-green body. The characteristic 'saw' contains 24–34 pairs of teeth. These teeth grow throughout the sawfish's life, but if they are lost, they are not re-grown. The body is elongated and flattened, with large, triangular pectoral fins and conspicuous dorsal fins. This bottom-living species is found in bays, lagoons, estuaries and occasionally rivers. It is known to be aggressive to sharks, which it strikes with its saw. The sawfish does well in aquaria.

Size Up to 7.6 m.
Distribution Widely scattered, circumglobal in tropical coastal waters.
Food Mostly slow-moving schooling fish, which are damaged with swipes of the saw. Digs for crabs and shellfish using the snout.

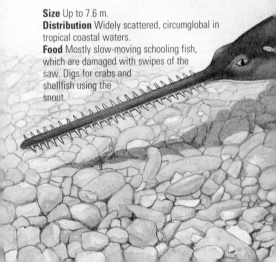

Breeding Live-bearer, with up to 15 or 20 young per litter.
Danger to humans Not known to be dangerous, but is a large powerful fish that should be treated with caution.

Sawfish

Electric Rays & Numbfish

Varying in size, electric rays and numbfish (Torpediniformes) are found inshore and offshore in all temperate and tropical seas, worldwide. The round or oval flabby disc and 2 dorsal fins are characteristic of this group. They are able to deliver an electric shock of up to 220 volts from 2 kidney-shaped organs behind the eyes. They eat mostly fish, which they catch either by lying in ambush or by using the electric organ to stun their prey. The majority of electric rays and numbfish are of no commercial value. Great care should be taken when handling these species.

Marbled Electric Ray *Torpedo marmorata*

This electric ray has a distinctive round, pale brown body with red-brown markings. It is active and solitary and when threatened can give a severe electric shock up to 220 volts. It lives in sea grass beds and over soft sea floor adjacent to reefs.

Size Up to 60 cm.
Distribution North-eastern Atlantic to S Africa and Mediterranean.
Food Mostly bony fish, including conger eel and bass, occasionally crabs and squid.
Breeding Live-bearer, with up to 32 young per litter.
Danger to humans Dangerous to bathers and fishermen who may receive an electric shock when fish is touched.

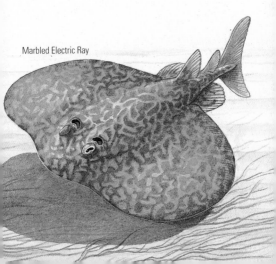

Marbled Electric Ray

ELECTRIC RAY *Torpedo nobiliana*

A large electric ray, uniformly black, brown or even dark purple. It has the characteristic round body and large dorsal and tail fins. This bottom-living species occurs to depths of 450 m where it is found over soft and gravel-like sea floors. Adults spend more time swimming than juveniles.

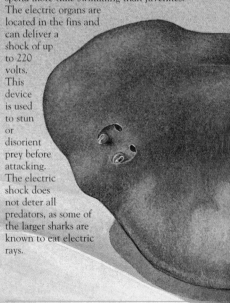

The electric organs are located in the fins and can deliver a shock of up to 220 volts. This device is used to stun or disorient prey before attacking. The electric shock does not deter all predators, as some of the larger sharks are known to eat electric rays.

Size Up to 1.8 m.
Distribution Temperate Atlantic waters.
Food Mainly bottom-living fish.
Breeding Live-bearer, with litters of up to 60 young.
Danger to humans If disturbed or handled can deliver a severe electric shock.

Electric Ray

COFFIN RAY *Hypnos monopterygium*

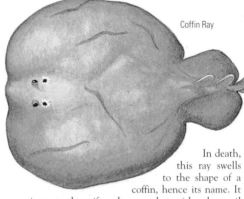

Coffin Ray

In death, this ray swells to the shape of a coffin, hence its name. It is a smooth, uniform brown colour with a short tail and very large disc. This species is found from the shore to depths of 240 m. It prefers sand and mud in grass beds and sandy patches in coral or rocky reefs. It is not a strong swimmer and in the daytime lies completely buried except for the spiracles.

Size Up to 69 cm.
Distribution Tropical and warm temperate Australia.
Food Bony fish, sea snails, shellfish and worms.
Breeding Live-bearer, gives birth in the summer.
Danger to humans Can deliver an electric shock if handled, but this is not fatal.

LESSER ELECTRIC RAY *Narcine brasiliensis*

A small electric ray with an almost circular disc. The body may be many shades of brown, and may or may not have dark markings. This species is nocturnal, lying buried during the day. It is common along sandy shorelines and sometimes near coral reefs where it disturbs its prey in the sand by flapping its disc.

Size Up to 45 cm.
Distribution S Carolina, USA to Argentina.
Food Worms, anemones and small shellfish.
Breeding Live-bearer, with litters of 2–17 young.
Danger to humans Can deliver an electric shock if handled.

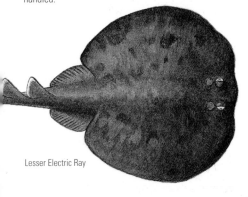

Lesser Electric Ray

TASMANIAN ELECTRIC RAY *Narcine tasmaniensis*

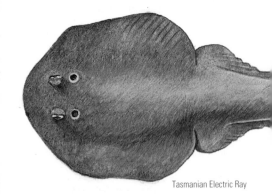

Tasmanian Electric Ray

A uniformly yellow or brown electric ray with a shovel-shaped disc that is shorter than the tail. The skin is smooth or wrinkled. It is commonly found on sand and mud throughout its range, and sometimes near reefs, mostly at depths of between 5 and 100 m.

Size Up to 46 cm.
Distribution South-eastern Australia.
Food Shrimps and worms.
Breeding Not known.
Danger to humans Can deliver an electric shock, but this is weak compared to other species.

BANDED NUMBFISH *Narcine westraliensis*

A distinctive numbfish with wide brown and yellow bands alternating over the body. The disc is small and circular and shorter than the tail. It lives on sand and mud on the continental shelf.

Size Up to 29 cm.
Distribution Western Australia.
Food Bottom-living worms and small invertebrates.
Breeding Main mating occurs September to October.
Danger to humans Can deliver an electric shock.

Banded Numbfish

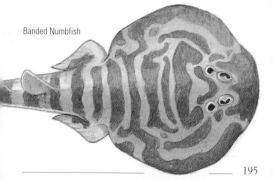

Rays & Skates

The terms ray and skate are interchangeable, but skate is usually used for those with longer snouts. This group (Rajiformes) contains some large rays, but the majority do not reach more than 1 m across the disc. They are found worldwide in marine and occasionally estuarine waters. They all have discs with a slender tail and many have spines on the back. They swim with a flapping motion of the fins and mainly feed on bottom-living creatures. Many are abundant, commercially important and are eaten by humans. This group is not known to be dangerous to people, but care should be taken when handling species with spines.

Spinetail Ray *Bathyraja spinicauda*

A large, grey ray with a long snout and relatively short tail. The upper surface is covered with prickles, but only the dorsal fin and tail have thorns. It is common in arctic and temperate seas at depths of between 140 and 800 m and at temperatures below 7.5°C.

Size Up to 1.7 m.
Distribution Newfoundland, Greenland, northern N Sea
to the Barents Sea.
Food A variety of bottom-living creatures.
Breeding Lays eggs, probably during summer.
Danger to humans Not known to be dangerous.

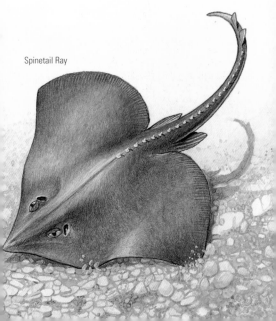

Spinetail Ray

Peacock Skate *Pavoraja nitida*

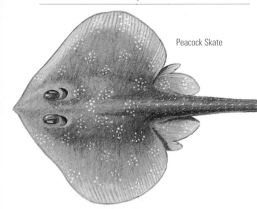

Peacock Skate

A small, heart-shaped skate with fine, white, clustered spots on a brown body. Very abundant on the continental shelf within its range and found at depths of between 30 and 390 m.

Size Up to 35 cm.
Distribution South-eastern Australia.
Food Not known.
Breeding Not known.
Danger to humans Not known to be dangerous.

COMMON SKATE *Raja batis*

A large, brown skate with either light spots or dusky blotches. There may be an eye-spot on the pectoral fin in immature fish. It is found between coastal waters to depths of 600 m, but mainly to 200 m. A commercial species that has declined owing to overfishing. The large size has earned it the nickname Barn Door Skate.

Size Up to 2.5 m; males are smaller than females.
Distribution NE Atlantic.
Food Bottom-living animals and fish.
Breeding Lays very large eggs in spring and summer.
Danger to humans Not known to be dangerous.

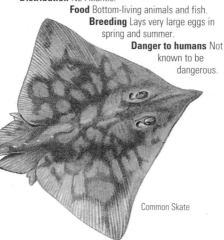

Common Skate

THORNBACK RAY _Raja clavata_

A large, prickly ray with a row of thorns from behind the head to the first dorsal fin, and large thorns scattered on the surface. The upper surface is grey or brown, and the pattern is variable. It is common on sand, mud, gravel and in rocky areas. It prefers shallow water between 2 and 60 m, but has been recorded to depths of 500 m. The breeding grounds of this species are inshore, the females arriving at these sites weeks before the males. A very important commercial species in northern Europe.

Thornback Ray

Size Up to 90 cm.
Distribution Atlantic coasts and Mediterranean.
Food Bottom-living animals, preferring shellfish.
Breeding Lays about 150 eggs each year. The embryo develops in about 5 months.
Danger to humans Not known to be dangerous.

BLONDE RAY *Raja brachyura*

The Blonde Ray is identified by its relatively large size, and particularly by the spots spreading right to the edge of the disc. The upper surface is covered in prickles and light blotches that may be circled by small dark spots. This common, inshore species is found to depths of 100 m, preferring a sandy sea floor.

Blonde Ray

Size Up to 1.2 m.
Distribution Temperate NE Atlantic coasts.
Food A variety of bottom-living animals.
Breeding Lays about 30 egg cases in spring and summer.
Danger to humans Not known to be dangerous.

CLEARNOSE SKATE *Raja eglanteria*

A medium-sized, grey skate with a pointed nose
and a single row of thorns running down the
middle of the back, starting between the shoulders
and ending at the tail. This common species is
often found close inshore, but occurs to depths of
120 m. It migrates north in summer and moves
offshore in hot weather.

Size Up to 75 cm.
Distribution Western Atlantic between Florida and
Massachusetts, USA.
Food Not known.
Breeding Not known.
Danger to humans Not known to be dangerous.

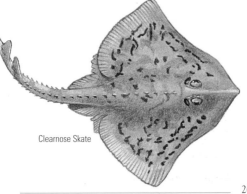

Clearnose Skate

LITTLE SKATE *Raja erinacea*

A small, grey or brown skate very similar to the Winter Skate (p. 210), but without eye-spots. This species lives over sand and gravel to depths of 150 m. It prefers deeper water in summer and shallow water in winter where it has been known to strand on shores in rough weather. It is sometimes called the Tobacco Box or Hedgehog Skate.

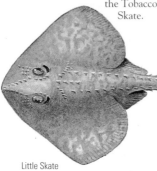

Little Skate

Size Up to 50 cm.
Distribution Western Atlantic, N Carolina to Nova Scotia.
Food Shellfish, shrimps, bristleworms, sea snails and fish.
Breeding Mates and lays eggs all year round, but is believed to have a low reproductive capacity.
Danger to humans Not known to be dangerous.

SHAGREEN RAY *Raja fullonica*

This large ray is recognised by the pronounced pointed snout and a spiny upper surface that is ash-grey in colour. There are 8 thorns on the inner edge of each eye. A relatively common species in cold waters on the upper edges of continental slopes at depths of between 30 and 550 m. It has a distinct preference for rough ground.

Size Up to 1 m.
Distribution Atlantic coasts from N Africa to Iceland and north to Russia.
Food Bottom-living animals and fish.
Breeding Lays egg cases that are 80 by 50 mm (excluding horns).
Danger to humans Not known to be dangerous.

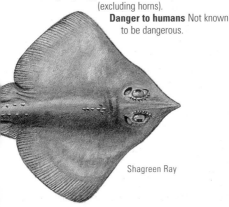

Shagreen Ray

ROUND RAY *Raja fyllae*

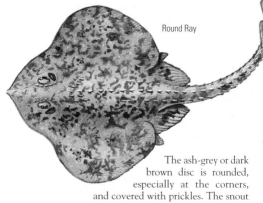

Round Ray

The ash-grey or dark brown disc is rounded, especially at the corners, and covered with prickles. The snout is very short and the tail may have dark bars. It is restricted to temperatures between 1 and 7°C at depths of between 170 and 2050 m.

Size Up to 55 cm.
Distribution N Atlantic coasts from northern France to Spitsbergen and west to Nova Scotia.
Food Bottom-living animals, especially invertebrates.
Breeding Lays small eggs.
Danger to humans Not known to be dangerous.

ARCTIC SKATE *Raja hyperborea*

This skate has a thick, flabby body and a short tail. The upper surface is dark grey or brown and is patchily covered in prickles, adults having more bare patches. This moderately common skate is restricted to water temperatures of -1–1.5°C and found at depths of between 300 and 1500 m.

Size Up to 85 cm.
Distribution Northern Atlantic from Norway northwards.
Food Bottom-living animals.
Breeding Lays eggs.
Danger to humans Not known to be dangerous.

Arctic Skate

SMALLEYED RAY *Raja microocellata*

The eyes on this ray are conspicuously small and the body is grey, white or light brown with light blotches and long stripes running parallel with the edges of the disc. A relatively common species found on sandy sea floors from inshore waters to depths of about 100 m.

Size Up to 80 cm.
Distribution Atlantic coasts from northern Africa to Ireland.
Food Bottom-living animals.
Breeding Lays eggs.
Danger to humans Not known to be dangerous.

Smalleyed Ray

CUCKOO RAY _Raja naevus_

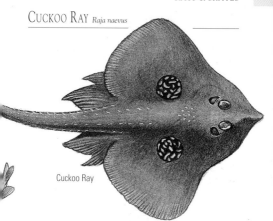

Cuckoo Ray

The body is brown-olive to pale grey-brown and there are large, black, round eye-spots and yellow wavy stripes in the middle of each of the pectoral fins. These markings are conspicuous. It is commonly encountered in coastal waters at depths of between 20 and 150 m.

Size Up to 70 cm.
Distribution Atlantic coasts from N Africa to southern Norway.
Food Bottom-living animals.
Breeding Lays eggs throughout the year.
Danger to humans Not known to be dangerous.

Winter Skate *Raja ocellata*

There are between 1 and 4 eye-spots edged in white on each pectoral fin and pale edged spots scattered over the brown back. A common species on sand and gravel often close inshore, especially in winter. It may occur offshore if temperatures rise and has been recorded migrating up to 16 km along coasts.

Size Up to 80 cm.
Distribution Western Atlantic from Newfoundland to N Carolina.
Food Bottom-living animals.
Breeding Lays eggs.
Danger to humans
Not known to be
dangerous.

Winter Skate

LONGNOSED SKATE *Raja oxyrinchus*

This angular skate has a long, pointed nose and wings with pointed corners. The upper surface is grey or dusky brown, smooth and spotty. It is a relatively common species, occurring on the sea floor at depths of between 90 and 900 m, but most often at about 200 m.

Size Up to 1.5 m.
Distribution NE Atlantic.
Food Bottom-living animals.
Breeding Lays eggs in spring and summer.
Danger to humans Not known to be dangerous.

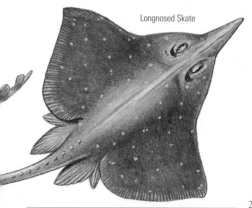

Longnosed Skate

STARRY SKATE *Raja radiata*

This skate has very large thorns on the upper surface, often with rosettes of black dots. The underside is white and occasionally has dark blotches. This common, bottom-living fish is found in coastal waters to depths of 1000 m, but mostly at 50–100 m. It is important in commercial catches.

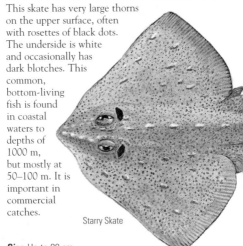

Starry Skate

Size Up to 90 cm.
Distribution In northern and arctic seas in the N Atlantic south to the English Channel and on the west coast to S Carolina.
Food Bottom-living animals.
Breeding Lays eggs.
Danger to humans Not known to be dangerous.

SMOOTH SKATE *Raja senta*

The pointed snout, slender tail, and brown disc that is broader than long, are characteristics of this skate. Lines of spines run down the back, on the shoulders and the inner edges of each eye. This skate prefers soft offshore mud and clay, at depths of between 150 and 325 m.

Size Up to 61 cm.
Distribution NW Atlantic.
Food Shellfish.
Breeding Lays eggs.
Danger to humans Not known to be dangerous.

Smooth Skate

UNDULATE RAY *Raja undulata*

This round ray has a short snout and a grey, brown or olive body, usually covered with wavy dark bands and white, pearl-sized spots. The upper surface is rough with bare patches. A common species, preferring soft and sandy sea floor on the continental shelf to depths of 200 m. Also called the Painted Ray.

Undulate Ray

Size Up to 1 m.
Distribution Atlantic coasts from Morocco to southern Ireland.
Food Bottom-living animals.
Breeding Lays eggs between March and September.
Danger to humans Not known to be dangerous.

MELBOURNE RAY *Raja whitleyi*

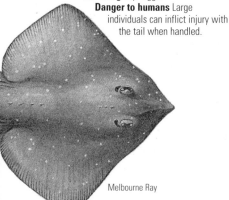

This large, broad-snouted ray has a comparatively short tail. The upper surface is rough and the underside is smooth, cream-coloured and occasionally has grey blotches. This ray has been recorded to depths of 170 m but is most abundant in shallow water.

Size Up to 1.7 m.
Distribution Southern Australia.
Food Not known, probably bottom-living animals.
Breeding Lays eggs.
Danger to humans Large individuals can inflict injury with the tail when handled.

Melbourne Ray

Guitarfish

Guitarfish (Rhinobatidae) are usually small to medium-sized, but the largest can reach 3 m. They are normally found near continental coastlines, but rarely near oceanic islands. The group is characterised by the shovel-shaped discs and long, flattened tails. They are found lying on the sea floor near reefs where they feed on shellfish and invertebrates. Although guitarfish are caught in bottom trawls, few are of commercial value. Members of this group are not dangerous to humans.

Eastern Shovelnose Ray *Aptychotrema rostrata*

This ray is either plain grey or brown or has dark blotches on a wedge-shaped disc. The long, triangular snout and curved mouth are characteristic of this species. It is commonly encountered on the sandy floors of bays, in the mouths of estuaries and off beaches. This active predator is also a scavenger and is often caught in nets and taken by anglers.

Size Up to 1.2 m.
Distribution South-western Australia.
Food Shellfish, sea snails and fish.
Breeding Live-bearer, with litters of up to 4 young.
Danger to humans Not known to be dangerous.

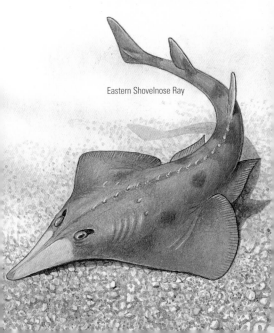

Eastern Shovelnose Ray

GUITARFISH *Rhinobatos rhinobatos*

This khaki-brown guitarfish has small spines running down the centre of the back from between the eyes to the tail. It swims slowly over sand and mud in which it buries itself when resting. It is sometimes found near rocky reefs. This species is found in shallow water to depths of 100 m.

Guitarfish

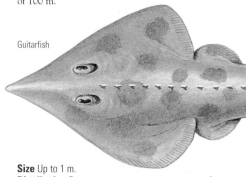

Size Up to 1 m.
Distribution Eastern Atlantic between Portugal and E Africa.
Food Mostly clams, squid and other bottom-living animals.
Breeding Live-bearer, with two litters of 4–10 young born each year.
Danger to humans Not known to be dangerous.

MAGPIE FIDDLER RAY *Trygonorrhina melaleuca*

This strikingly marked ray is only known from a
few specimens and may be a mutant. The bluish-
black upper surface and pale, irregularly shaped
patterns on the fin edges make it unmistakable.
Little is known about this rare, but beautiful, ray.

Size Up to 90 cm.
Distribution Restricted to a small area in S Australia.
Food Not known, probably bottom-living animals.
Breeding Not known.
Danger to humans Not known to be dangerous.

Magpie Fiddler Ray

SHARK RAY _Rhina ancylostoma_

Looking like a cross between a shark and a ray, this large, distinctively-shaped fish has heavy ridges on the head which, unlike that of other guitarfish, is visibly distinct from the fins. It is blue-grey with small white spots, but the colour fades as the animal grows. This fish is found in coastal areas, near coral reefs and wrecks and is a nuisance to prawn fishermen as it damages the catch when caught in trawls.

Shark Ray

Size Up to 2.7 m.
Distribution Widespread from E Africa to western Australia.
Food Crabs and shrimps.
Breeding Live-bearer, with 4 young per litter.
Danger to humans Not known to be dangerous.

WHITESPOTTED GUITARFISH *Rhynchobatus djiddensis*

A very stocky guitarfish with a triangular snout and pointed head. There are white spots down the sides of the grey or yellow-brown body and the tail is longer than the disc. This species occurs in the surf on beaches, in estuaries on sand, and near reefs.

Size Up to 3 m.
Distribution Widespread from E Africa to western Australia and north to Japan.
Food Crabs, lobsters, clams and small fish.
Breeding Live-bearer, with up to 10 young per litter.
Danger to humans Not dangerous, but will approach divers.

Whitespotted Guitarfish

Eagle, Cownose & Manta Rays, & Devilfish

This group (Myliobatiformes) contains the largest ray, the manta (p. 230), which can reach up to 9 m. Eagle rays have diamond-shaped heavy bodies with pectoral fins sited on the sides of the head below the eyes. Cownose rays are similar but have whip-like tails and can form massive schools. Manta rays and devilfish have prominent fleshy lobes on the front of the head that are extensions of the pectoral fins. They normally feed on a variety of fish and shellfish; the manta ray filter-feeds on plankton. The spines on the eagle and cownose rays should be treated with extreme care. Manta rays and devilfish are not dangerous to humans but are becoming increasingly shy of divers.

Spotted Eagle Ray *Aetobatus narinari*

A green to pink, white-spotted ray with a prominent head, angular pectoral fins and large, visible spiracles. The tail is whip-like and very long. This ray prefers reefs and often open ocean to depths of 60 m, but is occasionally found in estuaries. Extremely agile and powerful, it often leaps into the air. A strong fighter when hooked.

Size Up to 3.3 m.
Distribution Circumglobal in warm temperate and tropical seas.
Food Shellfish.
Breeding Live-bearer, with up to 4 young per litter.
Danger to humans Stings at the tail base and powerful jaws means this ray should be handled with care.

Spotted Eagle Ray

EAGLE RAY *Myliobatis aquila*

A dark brown or black ray with no distinctive markings, but the head is prominent and flat on top. The dorsal fin is set well back on the tail and has a large spine. This is a coastal species that enters estuaries but can occur to depths of 300 m. It is a strong swimmer, which leaps out of the water and is considered a good sporting fish by anglers.

Size Up to 1.5 m (disc width).
Distribution NE Atlantic, Mediterranean to S Africa.
Food Crabs and fish.
Breeding Live-bearer, with litters of 3–7 young.

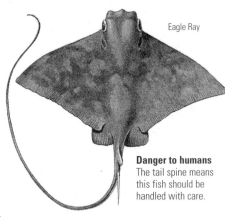

Eagle Ray

Danger to humans
The tail spine means this fish should be handled with care.

BULL RAY *Pteromylaeus bovinus*

A strikingly-patterned brown or black ray with bars that are visible when the fish is young, excited or injured. The head is prominent and the tail long and whip-like. A lively fish , which leaps from the water and is often hooked by sports anglers from the shore.

Size Up to 1.75 m (disc width).
Distribution Eastern Atlantic, Mediterranean to southern Africa.
Food Fish, crabs, bivalves and squid.
Breeding Live-bearer, with litters of 3–7 young.
Danger to humans Should be handled with care.

Bull Ray

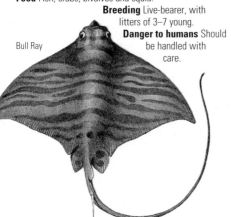

SOUTHERN EAGLE RAY *Myliobatis australis*

The olive-green or yellow disc of this eagle ray is smooth and very broad. The head is thick and prominent. It is a shallow water species, known to undergo local migrations, and is most commonly found off beaches and over sandflats. A powerful fish, which fights when hooked.

Size Up to 1.2 m (disc width).
Distribution S Australia.
Food Shellfish and crabs.
Breeding Live-bearer.
Danger to humans Not known to be dangerous.

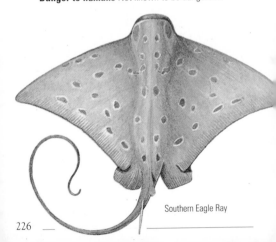

Southern Eagle Ray

SOUTHERN BAT RAY *Myliobatis tentuicaudatus*

Normally grey-green with blue bars and blotches, rare individuals of this species are orange with grey-green blotches. It lives in estuaries and bays on the sea floor where it has been observed 'blowing' water through the mouth and gills downwards, creating a hole to expose its prey.

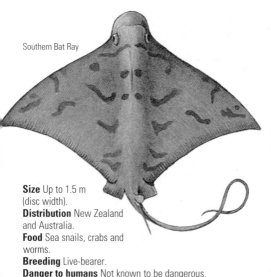

Southern Bat Ray

Size Up to 1.5 m
(disc width).
Distribution New Zealand
and Australia.
Food Sea snails, crabs and
worms.
Breeding Live-bearer.
Danger to humans Not known to be dangerous.

LUSITANIAN COWNOSE RAY *Rhinoptera marginata*

An indented head and swept-back, pointed pectoral fins are features of this cownose ray. The smooth skin is green-brown to bronze and the tail is long and whip-like. This fish is moderately common in warm waters, often forming large groups, and has been seen swimming at the surface.

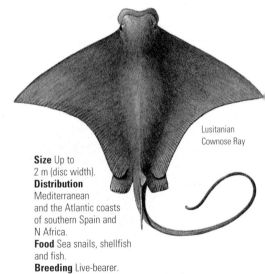

Lusitanian
Cownose Ray

Size Up to
2 m (disc width).
Distribution
Mediterranean
and the Atlantic coasts
of southern Spain and
N Africa.
Food Sea snails, shellfish
and fish.
Breeding Live-bearer.
Danger to humans Not known to be dangerous.

AUSTRALIAN COWNOSE RAY *Rhinoptera neglecta*

This ray has a uniformly dark brown or grey, stocky body. The forehead, with two distinct bulges, and short, whip-like tail are characteristic of this species. It is known to occur in bays and estuaries.

Size Up to 86 cm (disc width).
Distribution Eastern Australia.
Food Clams, oysters and other shellfish.
Breeding Live-bearer.
Danger to humans Not known to be dangerous.

Australian Cownose Ray

MANTA RAY *Manta birostris*

This enormous ray is one of the largest living fish. It is grey-blue to green-brown above, sometimes with paler patches on the shoulders. The underside is white with grey edges. The distinctive paddle-shaped flaps on the head and the very broad mouth (without teeth) act as a funnel, and special gills sieve out plankton. The body surface is rough and the tail is short and spineless.

Manta Ray

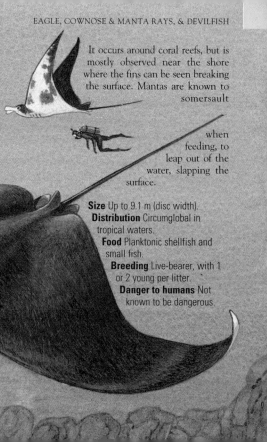

It occurs around coral reefs, but is mostly observed near the shore where the fins can be seen breaking the surface. Mantas are known to somersault when feeding, to leap out of the water, slapping the surface.

Size Up to 9.1 m (disc width).
Distribution Circumglobal in tropical waters.
Food Planktonic shellfish and small fish.
Breeding Live-bearer, with 1 or 2 young per litter.
Danger to humans Not known to be dangerous.

JAPANESE DEVIL RAY *Mobula japanica*

A blue devil ray with white-tipped dorsal fin and shoulder patches. The whip-like tail has white thorn-like denticles on each side and a stinging spine. This fish is either solitary or occurs in small groups in surface waters.

Size Up to 3.1 m (disc width).
Distribution Probably circumglobal in tropical waters.
Food Planktonic shellfish.

Breeding Live-bearer, only 1 young per litter.
Danger to humans Not known to be dangerous.

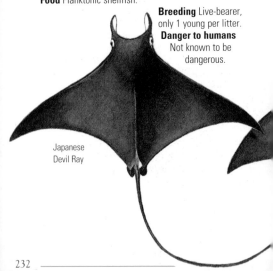

Japanese
Devil Ray

DEVILFISH *Mobula mobular*

A devilfish with the head elevated from the brown or black disc and eyes and spiracle sited on the side. The short, whip-like tail is distinct from the disc and has a spine. This fish swims in the open water, often in pairs or groups, and is only occasionally seen near the shore.

Size Up to 5.2 m (disc width).
Distribution Tropical and warm temperate waters, and oceanic islands.
Food Fish and shellfish.
Breeding Live-bearer, with 1 or 2 young per litter.
Danger to humans The jagged spines on the top of the tail should be handled with care.

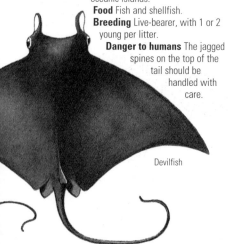

Devilfish

STINGRAYS, STINGAREES & BUTTERFLY RAYS

Stingrays (Myliobatiformes) can reach 3 m or more (disc width). They do not have dorsal fins and the skin is smooth and variable in colour. The head is elevated above the pectoral fins and the tail is long and whip-like with a sting enveloped in venomous tissue. Stingarees have a shorter, slender tail and the head is not raised. Butterfly rays are very flat, butterfly-wing-shaped rays. The head is continuous with the body. Stingrays prefer calm, shallow water when they bury in mud and sand. They feed on a variety of bottom-living creatures and can seriously damage shellfish culturing areas. The stingrays are of no commercial importance. In defending itself a stingray will lash its tail at an attacker. Wounds often require stitching, and although the pain is intense, and can paralyse, it rarely results in death.

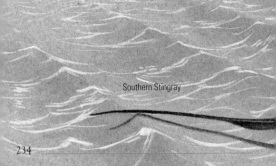

Southern Stingray

Southern Stingray *Dasyatis americana*

The rounded disc is a uniform grey or brown with no markings. This species is found on sandy sea floors and near reef faces where it is active at night, but lies buried during the day. The tail, which has a sting in a venomous sheath, is used in defence.

Size Up to 1.5 m (disc width).
Distribution Western Atlantic.
Food Fish, crabs and worms.
Breeding Live-bearer, with 3–5 young per litter.
Danger to humans Can be handled by divers, but will bite or raise the tail and sting over the body if harassed.

STINGRAY *Dasyatis pastinaca*

A distinctive grey or brown stingray with a disc that is broad at the front, tapering to the tail, which ends in a long, thin whip. The upper surface is smooth, but there are thorns on the top of the tail. The tail contains a jagged spine that is used for defence when disturbed or threatened. This species is commonly found in calm and shallow water on sand and mud and near reefs, to depths of 200 m. They can tolerate some amounts of freshwater, and are occasionally found in estuaries. Some may be found with two spines, as replacements grow before the old spines are lost. In Greek mythology, Ulysses was reputedly killed with a spear tipped with a stingray spine.

Stingray

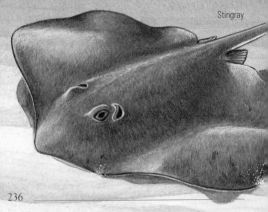

Size Up to 60 cm (disc width).
Distribution Atlantic coasts.
Food Bottom-living invertebrates and fish.
Breeding Live-bearer, with 4–7 young per litter.
Danger to humans The spine can be lifted up over the body, like a scorpion, and cause injury.

Roughtail Stingray *Dasyatis centroura*

The large disc is yellow to olive-green with a slightly wavy front edge. The tail is ridged, very long and has 1 or more poisonous spines sited towards the base. This fish is not very common, but is found on mud and sand in shallow water. It is usually found nearer coasts in the summer.

Size Up to 3 m (disc width).
Distribution Eastern and western Atlantic.
Food Bottom-living animals.
Breeding Live-bearer.
Danger to humans This fish should be handled with care, as the spine can cause injury.

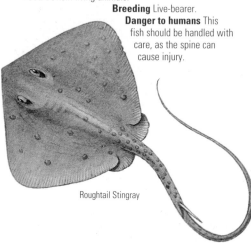

Roughtail Stingray

HONEYCOMB STINGRAY *Himantura uarnak*

A beautifully patterned stingray. The back is black or brown and there are cream or yellow spots, bars and patterns. The tail is long, black and whip-like. Like all stingrays, the tail has a spine. Young specimens have dense black spots and a banded tail. It occurs from the shoreline to depths of 45 m.

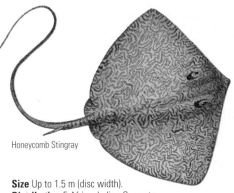

Honeycomb Stingray

Size Up to 1.5 m (disc width).
Distribution E Africa, Indian Ocean to Australia. Recently recorded in the Mediterranean, entering via the Suez Canal.
Food A variety of bottom-living and mid-water prey.
Breeding Live-bearer, with 1–5 young per litter.
Danger to humans This fish should be handled with care, as the spine can cause injury.

MANGROVE WHIP RAY *Himantura granulata*

This oval-shaped ray is uniformly dark brown or grey and usually studded with light flecks. The tail is long, white, whip-like and may contain 1 or more stinging spines. Little is known of this stingray, which occurs in mangrove areas.

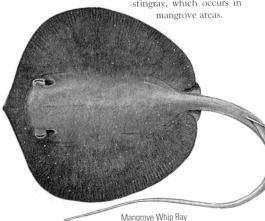

Mangrove Whip Ray

Size Up to 90 cm (disc width), possibly larger.
Distribution Western Indo-Pacific.
Food Crabs and prawns.
Breeding Live-bearer.
Danger to humans This fish should be handled with care, as the spine can cause injury.

BLUESPOTTED RIBBONTAIL RAY *Taeniura lymma*

This small, beautiful, blue-spotted ray has 2 stings in a relatively short, striped tail. It is abundant around coral reefs, and is known to migrate into shallow sandy areas where it feeds as the tide rises. It rarely buries itself.

Size Up to 30 cm (disc width).
Distribution Western Indo-Pacific.
Food Worms, crabs and bony fish.
Breeding Live-bearer, with up to 7 young in a litter.
Danger to humans This fish should be handled with care, as the spine can cause injury.

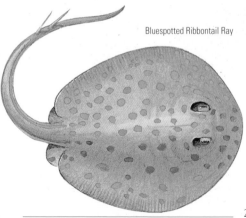

Bluespotted Ribbontail Ray

YELLOW STINGAREE *Urolophus jamaicensis*

A small, spotty, blotchy-patterned ray that has a tail shorter than the disc. It occurs in harbours and bays where it has been observed flapping the pectoral fins over the sandy sea floor to expose buried prey. It also lifts the front to form a cave into which shelter-seeking prey are attracted.

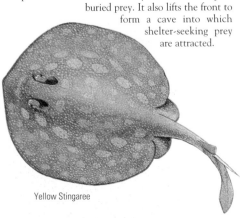

Yellow Stingaree

Size Up to 67 cm (disc width).
Distribution Gulf of Mexico and Caribbean.
Food Shrimps and fish.
Breeding There are 2–4 young in a litter.
Danger to humans This fish should be handled with care.

CIRCULAR STINGAREE *Urolophus circularis*

A large, blue-grey stingaree with pale spots, blotches and rings. It has a fleshy snout, large eyes and a short, rounded tail. This fish is not common, but it is observed on reefs, rocky sea bed and in seaweed.

Size Up to 60 cm.
Distribution South-western Australia.
Food Not known.
Breeding Live-bearer, with 2–4 young per litter.
Danger to humans No records of humans being injured.

Circular Stingaree

BANDED STINGAREE *Urolophus cruciatus*

A distinctively patterned grey to yellow-brown stingaree with dark bars over the body. The tail is short, flattened and has a jagged spine. This species prefers muddy sea floors in estuaries and bays, where it lies buried.

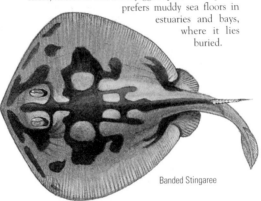

Banded Stingaree

Size Up to 60 cm.
Distribution SE Australia.
Food Probably bottom-living animals.
Breeding Live-bearer, with 2–4 young per litter.
Danger to humans This species has a very flexible tail which can reach any part of its body. A spine broken in a wound will need surgery.

Smooth Butterfly Ray *Gymnura micrura*

A very flat, smooth, butterfly-shaped ray with a short tail. The colouring changes with its background. The tail is ridged and has bars but there is no spine. This ray is found in shallow, sometimes brackish, water, and is known to move with the tide.

Size Up to 60 cm (disc width).
Distribution Western Atlantic.
Food Not known, probably bottom-living animals.
Breeding Live-bearer, with 2–6 young per litter.
Danger to humans Not known to be dangerous.

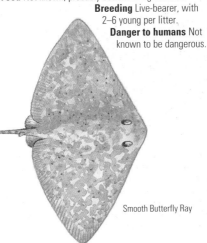

Smooth Butterfly Ray

AUSTRALIAN BUTTERFLY RAY *Gymnura australis*

An attractive green-grey or yellow ray with a peppering of black spots. It has a short, black and white banded, spineless tail. The snout is angular with a fleshy lobe. This inshore species is found at depths to 50 m and is caught by prawn trawlers. An edible fish, which is sometimes sold as skate.

Australian Butterfly Ray

Size Up to 73 cm (disc width).
Distribution Northern Australia.
Food Not known, probably bottom-living animals.
Breeding Live-bearer, with 2–6 young per litter.
Danger to humans Not known to be dangerous.

Further Reading

Budker, P. 1971. *The Life of Sharks*. London, Ebenezer Baylis & Son.

Compagno, L.J.V. 1984. FAO Species Catalogue Vol. 4. Parts I and II. *Sharks of the World. An Annotated and Illustrated Catalogue of Shark Species Known to Date*. Rome. Food and Agriculture Organisation of the United Nations.

Gilbert, P. (ed). 1963. *Sharks and Survival*. Boston, Heath & Co.

Last, P.R. & Stevens, J.D. 1994. *Sharks and Rays of Australia*. Australia, CSIRO.

Michael, S.W. 1993. *Reef Sharks and Rays of the World. A guide to their identification, behaviour and ecology*. California, USA, Sea Challengers.

Randall, J.E. 1968. *Caribbean Reef Fishes.* Jersey City, USA. Tropical Fish Hobbyist.

Whitehead, P.J.P., Bauchot, M.L., Hureau, J.C., Nielsen, J. & Tortonese, E. (eds). 1984-1986. *Fishes of the north-eastern Atlantic and the Mediterranean*. Vols I-III. Paris, UNESCO.

Glossary

Anal fin Fin behind the anus.

Atoll A circular reef with a central lagoon resting on top of a submerged volcano.

Barbel A tentacle-like protuberance or growth under the nose or chin, which has taste cells to detect prey.

Breaching When an animal jumps partially or totally out of the water.

Cartilage Soft, white, gristle-like skeletal material.

Continental shelf The sea bed adjacent to the coast extending to a depth of 200 m.

Continental slope Steep-sloping sea bed bordering the continental shelf, extending to depths of 2000 m.

Circumglobal Distributed around the globe within defined latitudes.

Deep-water Below depths of 200 m.

Denticles Small thorn-like scales totally or partially covering a shark's body.

Disc The combined head, trunk and pectoral fins of a skate or ray.

Dorsal The back or upper surface of the body.

Dorsal fin Fin or fins on the back of the shark or ray.

Filter-feeding Filtering food particles floating in the water by means of the gill rakers.

Gestation Retaining and nourishing the young in the female's reproductive tract.

Gills Folds of skin in the head that extract oxygen from the water.

Gill filaments Individual projections within the gills that provide a large surface area for the extraction of oxygen.

Gill net A net used to catch sharks and rays by their gills.

Gill rakers Projections attached to an arch in the gills.

Gill slits Narrow openings on the head through which water is expelled.

Invertebrates Animals without backbones, e.g. crabs, squid and mussels.

Keel A fleshy ridge, usually just in front of the tail, used as a stabiliser when the shark is in motion.

Krill Shrimp-like plankton.

Lateral line Line of sensory cells running down the body that locate moving animals at short range by the disturbance of water.

Live-bearing Gives birth to live young.

Lobes Round protuberances growing on the body.

Mid-water Living below the surface and above the sea floor.

Nasal Pertaining to the nostrils.

Nasal flaps Skin flaps over the nostrils.

Nocturnal Active at night.

Nursery areas Places, usually near the coast, where young sharks feed and grow.

Pectoral fins A pair of fins behind or below the gill opening. These are not distinct from the body in skates and rays.

Pelvic fins A pair of fins under the body behind the pectoral fins.

Plankton Small animals and plants that float in the water and drift with water currents. An important food source for some sharks and rays.

School Collective term for groups of sharks or rays that swim in close association.

Sex-segregation Males and females occur in separate groups.

Spine A sharp, projecting point.

Spiracle Respiratory vent or opening behind the eyes, through which seawater is taken in.

Tubercles Hard or soft projections on the head or body.

Uterine cannibalism One pup eats others while in the female's reproductive tract (uterus).

Wings The pectoral fins of skates and rays, which look and flap like wings.

INDEX